Breakfast with Yeshua

A Messianic Jewish Devotional

D.C. Harris

© 2022

Copyright © 2022 by David Chapman Harris

All rights reserved.

No part of this publication may be reproduced, stored in a retrieval system, or transmitted in any form or by any means – for example, electronic, photocopy, recording – without prior written permission from the author / owner. The only exception is brief quotations in book reviews.

www.BeatGoliath.com

Scripture quotations marked CSB have been taken from the Christian Standard Bible®, Copyright © 2017 by Holman Bible Publishers. Used by permission. Christian Standard Bible® and CSB® are federally registered trademarks of Holman Bible Publishers.

Library of Congress Control Number: 2020907440

Cover Photograph: Jason Villanueva

ISBN: 979-8-2241-1181-7

For Hadassah
Always remembering what is most important…

Faith, Hope, & Love

I must not neglect to express my gratitude to the good people of *Adat Yeshua Messianic Synagogue.* Without you amazing Adatniks this book could not have been written. *Thank you!*

May God continue to bless us, and knit each of us together as one in the Messiah.

<u>JANUARY 1</u>

Welcome to a new year! Find a solitary place where you can seek the Lord and make this time sacred. Sit quietly and take a deep breath. Ask God to enter into your thoughts, and grant you his peace.

If you are in Yeshua, he is also inside of you. His word testifies to this, and during his ministry on earth his miracles were meant to testify to the same thing – he lives inside you. When your heart is still, read his word slowly and carefully. In this passage, consider how he tried to persuade those who stood against him…

If I am not doing my Father's works, don't believe me. But if I am doing them and you don't believe me, believe the works. This way you will know and understand that the Father is in me and I in the Father."

✡ *John 10:37-38*

The greatest miracle for those who are in Yeshua is that he takes up residence within us, just like the Father dwells in him. He is The One living inside our hearts. There is no greater miracle than this!

In prayer and humility, ask Yeshua to bless this day, whatever may come. You might begin with, "Dear God, I am always and ever in need of you. Please sustain me today as I…"

JANUARY 2

Another new day brings another opportunity to walk with your blessed Savior. In your quite place make your heart still, and prepare your thoughts for what he has in store for you today.

As it also says in Hosea, I will call Not My People, My People, and she who is Unloved, Beloved.

✡ *Romans 9:25*

Are you thankful God sees you as you really are, not as others see you, or as you sometimes see yourself? Although we are all sinners, through the blood of Yeshua we are called 'loved ones' of God; we are his beloved people. This includes you.

Ponder this deeply, and when you are ready, pray, "Loving Heavenly Father, I rejoice that you have called me 'loved one.' Please help me to be more loving today, and allow me to bless others by…"

JANUARY 3

It is no secret that God knows all things. He has perfect vision and perspective on the past, present, and future. He understands every detail of all potentiality, and has exhaustive knowledge of your own life, as well as the lives of every creature that has ever lived on the earth. As such, he knows full well that his first children, the Jewish people, will be with him in the end, when all things are put to right.

I ask, then, has God rejected his people? Absolutely not! For I too am an Israelite, a descendant of Abraham, from the tribe of Benjamin. God has not rejected his people whom he foreknew.

✡ *Romans 11:1-2a*

It may look as if your Jewish friends and family are too distant, too far away from God to be care about Yeshua. But God is not far from anyone. Many people pass away and die out of time without leaving a clear understanding of their faith for those of us who remain to consider what may come of them in the afterworld. But never fear. God knows.

Ask him today for peace in your own heart, and trust him to take care of the future.

JANUARY 4

Another day to do battle! Are you ready?

Paul the Apostle lets us know, just as the prophets of old did, that there will come a day of permanent and final judgment. The Day of the Lord will be a joy for some, and simultaneously a disaster for others, all at once. With Yeshua as your Savior you can take great comfort in the fact that your final destination is the Kingdom of Heaven.

But Isaiah cries out concerning Israel: Though the number of Israelites is like the sand of the sea, only the remnant will be saved; since the Lord will execute his sentence completely and decisively on the earth.

✡ *Romans 9:27-28*

Pray like so: "Dear Lord, please walk with me today through this dangerous world, and allow me to live my life for your glory. Please help the following people whom I love…"

<u>JANUARY 5</u>

How is your year going so far? In your place of prayer take stock for a moment and prepare yourself for what the Lord holds in store for you today. The future belongs to God!

And just as Isaiah predicted: If the Lord of Hosts had not left us offspring, we would have become like Sodom, and we would have been made like Gomorrah.

✡ *Romans 9:29*

Are you able to look back on your life with gratitude and thankfulness, knowing that God has caused you to thrive and grow? He is your merciful Heavenly Father, and he wants the very best for you. Consider the many good things God has done for you today. If you feel like you have been short changed, ask Yeshua to re-align your perspective.

You might begin your time in prayer with, "Loving Lord, sometimes I feel like I'm not getting anywhere, but I know you are trustworthy. One area of my life that really needs your help is…"

JANUARY 6

It is important to spend time in the presence of your Lord. Enter into that quiet place of prayer, close your eyes, take some deep breaths, and prepare to meditate on his word. It is nourishment for your soul…

Look, I am putting a stone in Zion to stumble over and a rock to trip over, and the one who believes on him will not be put to shame.

✡ *Romans 9:33*

When you put your faith in the Lord Yeshua and his crosswork, you can confidently trust in him; you will not be put to shame. Everybody you know may let you down, but he will never shame you.

"Dear Heavenly Father, I come to you today with a heart of gratitude. Thank you for your mercy and grace as I struggle with…"

<u>JANUARY 7</u>

As you prepare for another day, make it a point to carve out some quiet time to sit and ponder what the Lord has for you. Your Heavenly Father is always there to hear your prayers, always there to care for your needs.

Now some Greeks were among those who went up to worship at the festival. So they came to Philip, who was from Bethsaida in Galilee, and requested of him, "Sir, we want to see Jesus."

✡ *John 12:20-21*

This short phrase, "Sir, we want to see Jesus (or Yeshua!)," has been written on the pulpits of many Christian ministers throughout history, to remind preachers that people gather not to hear clever stories, but to see Christ. If you see the world *'through heaven's eyes,'* as the song says, you will find traces of God's handiwork everywhere you look.

You might begin your prayers today with, "Dear Lord, I wish to see the world through spiritual eyes. *I want to see Yeshua!* Help me to recognize the image of God in myself and in other people. Help me to love as he loved, and honor you today by…"

JANUARY 8

Welcome to a new day! Invite the Lord into your quiet time, and take a few moments to re-dedicate your heart to him. Even an ordinary week can become extraordinary when you ask the Lord to help you in the daily routines.

Jesus replied to them, "The hour has come for the Son of Man to be glorified. Truly I tell you, unless a grain of wheat falls to the ground and dies, it remains by itself. But if it dies, it produces much fruit.

✡ *John 12:23-24*

Yeshua embraced death so that we could inherit life. Amazingly, *that was his glory!* When you appreciate the great sacrifice which God has made of himself, the only proper response is to give him your own life. Do that today by thanking him, and praying along these lines, "Dear Lord, I am grateful that you have counted me as one of your 'seeds.' Please help me to further spread your good news by…"

<u>JANUARY 9</u>

There is no doubt that God is able to restore his people to faith. And if he can do that, he can rescue anybody. What's more, no people group on earth has had such an opportunity to know the living God as the Jewish people. If he can restore them by his grace, then he can bring *you* home too, along with all those people you love so dearly.

For if you were cut off from your native wild olive tree and against nature were grafted into a cultivated olive tree, how much more will these — the natural branches — be grafted into their own olive tree?

✡ *Romans 11:24*

Allow God to change you inwardly and outwardly, in whatever way he sees fit. In preparation for today, you might pray like so:

"Dear Lord, you know me better than anyone else does, and you know me better than I know myself. Please give me your blessing, and conform me to your holiness."

JANUARY 10

With each new day you draw one step closer to the Kingdom of God. Are you ready to do what the Lord calls you to, and go where he takes you? Make sure to clear your mind and heart of all the clutter, so that you can focus on the ministry he has set before you today. Read his word slowly…

If anyone serves me, he must follow me. Where I am, there my servant also will be. If anyone serves me, the Father will honor him.

✡ *John 12:26*

In the Bible, to be a *servant of God* is a very high honor. Bob Dylan wrote a song, "You gotta' serve somebody!" And it's very true! Who are *you* going to serve today? Many times we want to *be* served, but to be a servant of the King of Kings is the greatest post a person can ever hope for.

Ask God to make you his servant today by praying, "Dear Lord, I'm here to do what you have called me to. Guide me and teach me today as I…"

JANUARY 11

Begin your devotional time with a few deep breaths, close your eyes, and be still in your soul. Listen to the sound of your own heart beating, and give your thoughts to Yeshua. When you are ready, read.

"Now my soul is troubled. What should I say — Father, save me from this hour? But that is why I came to this hour. Father, glorify your name."

Then a voice came from heaven: "I have glorified it, and I will glorify it again."

✡ *John 12:27-28*

Sometimes we face incredibly difficult times which we simply cannot understand. It is easy during our most painful moments to think of God as unfair when all we see is trouble. But you can take comfort in the fact that Yeshua has taken full responsibility for the injustice of this world, by accepting his own destiny, to die on a cross for your sins.

Ask God to be glorified in you today: "Dear Lord, the weight of this world is too much for me to carry. Thankfully, I can ask you to help me with…"

JANUARY 12

Have things been rough lately? Take some quiet time to reflect on the past few days. What good has come of your efforts? In what areas do you need God's help to change? Enjoy the word of God...

Jesus answered, "The light will be with you only a little longer. Walk while you have the light so that darkness doesn't overtake you. The one who walks in darkness doesn't know where he's going. While you have the light, believe in the light so that you may become children of light." Jesus said this, then went away and hid from them.

✡ *John 12:35-36*

Earlier followers of Yeshua wrestled with the idea that they were 'children of light.' They built towering churches with great steeples and stained glass windows to let the light shine into their houses of worship. These grand structures stand all over Europe as testimony to the believers who came before us, and their desire to reflect the light of Yeshua.

How can you shine God's light in your personal life today? You might start by praying the following: "Dear Lord, please fill my heart and mind with your light. Help me see things as you see them, and to walk along with you. I praise you today because..."

<u>JANUARY 13</u>

You never know what the Lord may do with your day, so always begin with prayer. Set your focus on him, and prepare yourself for what he has in store for you. Your Heavenly Father is happy to meet you in your devotional time.

"Daughter Zion, shout for joy and be glad, for I am coming to dwell among you" — this is the Lord's declaration.

✡ *Zechariah 2:10*

The command to 'shout for joy' (to *rejoice*) is just as important as anything else the Lord would have you do. It is far too easy to get tied up in all the rules and regulations we think make God love us, but Yeshua loves us not because of what we *do*, but because of *who we are in him* – we are *his*! That's a good reason to be joyful.

Take time to give thanks to the Lord for all he has done for you, and to voice your concerns as well. "Heavenly Father, I rejoice and thank you for…"

<u>JANUARY 14</u>

Even though it may seem like just another morning, each day has eternal consequences. One day you will stand before the Lord, and if you have placed your trust in Yeshua, he will say to you, "Good job! Welcome home!" Spend some quiet time with you heavenly Father today.

"Many nations will join themselves to the Lord on that day and become my people. I will dwell among you, and you will know that the Lord of Armies has sent me to you.

✡ *Zechariah 2:11*

At some point, 'that day' which the prophets speak of will actually arrive. 'That day' is going to be overwhelmingly dreadful for many, and indescribably thrilling for others – *both at the same time*, because he comes as a warrior. The encroaching *Day of the Lord* is something the prophets have foretold, and which all believers in Yeshua can look forward to and prepare for. He will restore our broken world, and finish making all things new. Offer him your prayers in anticipation of his return.

<u>JANUARY 15</u>

The sovereign God is ruler of all things, even having mastery over chaos. His thoughts are far beyond our thoughts, and yet he invites us to come share our time with him whenever we wish. Take advantage of the opportunity to open up to your loving God today.

The Lord will take possession of Judah as his portion in the Holy Land, and he will once again choose Jerusalem.

✡ *Zechariah 2:12*

There is only one Jerusalem, and yet we are told in Scripture that someday the whole earth will be renewed, and a New Jerusalem will be at the center of the world, glorified and beautiful, free from all sin and death. When the children of Israel were brought out from Egypt into the Holy Land, the Lord was with them all the way. Likewise, he will be with you all the way too, as he brings you out of this fallen world and into his kingdom.

Today you might begin your prayers with, "Dear God, I want to be a part of your inheritance. Send me where you will, but please stay with me today as I…"

JANUARY 16

Sometimes we get caught up in the rat race, chasing our own tails, running around, and feeling dizzy. Take some time today, before you set foot out into the busy world, to meditate on the word of the Lord. He has a plan for you, and as you pray he will fill you with his strength and peace.

Let all people be silent before the Lord, for from his holy dwelling he has roused himself."

✡ *Zechariah 2:13*

In these crazy times it is important to seek the deeper, more meaningful life with Yeshua. That may mean changing old ways, and cultivating new habits. How can we ever learn to '*be still before the Lord,*' if we have a hard time being silent? It is important to turn off the noise, and simply listen to God. Before you pray, take several deep breaths, and close your eyes. Allow yourself to become more fully aware of the fact that God is holy and pure. When you are ready, share your heart with the Lord.

JANUARY 17

When you became a believer and follower of Yeshua, you entered into a spiritual war. Fortunately you serve a great God, the only God! And happily, he has already won the battle! Even still, there are all kinds of things that happen in the spiritual realms, 'behind the scenes' which we are unaware of. If you are ever afraid, you can know with certainty that God is there to be your advocate and friend. Consider the following amazing passage.

Then he showed me the high priest Joshua standing before the angel of the Lord, with Satan standing at his right side to accuse him The Lord said to Satan: "The Lord rebuke you, Satan! May the Lord who has chosen Jerusalem rebuke you! Isn't this man a burning stick snatched from the fire? "

✡ *Zechariah 3:1-2*

As a disciple of Yeshua, you too are a 'priest' of sorts, like Joshua was long ago. You may not wear a tunic, or a turban, and you may not work in a temple, church or synagogue, but your life is an honor dedicated to him, and he will stick up for you! Along with all the other believers worldwide and throughout history you can take comfort that you are on the winning side. Enter into the spiritual battlefield today by praying as the Lord would lead you.

JANUARY 18

Have you felt beat up, kicked, bruised, and knocked down? How can you make it through another day? Rely on your God, the Holy One who will see you through. Make time for him every day, and keep your eyes fixed on Yeshua, on his crosswork, and the promise of a bright future.

Now Joshua was dressed with filthy clothes as he stood before the angel.

✡ *Zechariah 3:3*

It may not seem like it now, but there will come a time when you will feel no more pain, or fatigue, or stress. Wouldn't that be wonderful? When you entrust your life to the nail-pierced hands of Yeshua, he gives you a destiny and a reason to hope for the days ahead. All the dirt and filth of this world will be washed away, and he will clothe you in fine garments of righteousness. You will be able to stand before God, and nobody will ever condemn you, or take away what he has given.

Praise him today for what he has done and will do in your life. "Dear Heavenly Father, I trust and adore you because you…"_

JANUARY 19

Many blessings for another morning! Are you ready for what God has in store for you? Get into the right frame of mind by quietly opening your heart up to the Lord. Your devotional time with him is precious, and will bring spiritual rewards.

Watch out, brothers and sisters, so that there won't be in any of you an evil, unbelieving heart that turns away from the living God.

✡ *Hebrews 3:12*

It may be that you have had to deal with some suffering lately, and if so, you may wonder where God is in all of this mess. See to it that you do not harden your heart against the Lord. He gives us a loving warning!

We are engaged in a spiritual battle, and there are times when we may question God's presence in our lives. Be sure to let him work deeply in your heart. Invite Yeshua into your entire day – awake or asleep, at work or play, wherever you may go.

A good way to start your prayers might be, "Loving Lord, I trust that you see me today, please make my heart more like yours, and please help me to become more like you in the following ways…"

JANUARY 20

As your life continues, remember to pray for those fellow believers who you might only see once per week, or hardly at all. Take time to call to mind your brothers and sisters in Yeshua who may be struggling this season.

But encourage each other daily, while it is still called today, so that none of you is hardened by sin's deception.

✡ *Hebrews 3:13*

You may not feel it all the time, but you need other believers in your life. We all do. If you head out on your own each day without taking time to check your heart with God, you may overlook some of the good things he is putting in your path. If you find yourself living two separate lives – one at work, the other in the sanctuary – ask your Heavenly Father to work on your heart.

You might pray along these lines: "Dear God, I do not want to behave differently in front of my co-workers, than in front of other believers. Please help me to grow in integrity, and encourage others by…"

JANUARY 21

Each day presents a new opportunity to learn, and walk with Yeshua. If you step out in faith, you can bank on him being there for you. If you stumble and fall, he will lift you up. You can put your trust entirely in him. Nobody else has ever died on a cross for your sins! And he loves to meet you in your prayer times.

For we have become participants in Christ if we hold firmly until the end the reality that we had at the start.

✡ *Hebrews 3:14*

Life is a marathon, not a sprint race. Sometimes we rise up in the morning singing, other times we have to drag ourselves out of bed. Do you remember the energy and excitement you had about your new-found faith, when you first became a believer in Yeshua? Do not allow the challenging times to rob you of the prize that awaits you in Heaven. As this verse of Scripture says, hold your confidence in Yeshua firmly *until the end!* This can only be done with his help, so pray with all your heart.

"Dear Lord, I need your help! I am having trouble lately with…"

JANUARY 22

The family of believers in Yeshua includes people from the ancient past, all the way into our times. And yet, God wants still more people to hear and receive the good news! Make your heart calm before him, take some deep breaths, and come to your God in humility. Read slowly each word…

For we have heard how the Lord dried up the water of the Red Sea before you when you came out of Egypt.

✡ *Joshua 2:10*

When God rescued the children of Israel from slavery, he told Moses to inform Pharaoh that plagues would fall on the Egyptian people, *so that they may know* there is a God looking after the Israelites. By the time Joshua was ready to take the city of Jericho the word had spread far and wide. People had heard of the reputation of the Lord, the God of Israel. Have the people in your life have heard enough already about the goodness of the Lord?

Maybe there is someone you know personally who would benefit from your brave compassion, and who needs to hear some encouragement. Pray about that today. If you don't tell the lost about the Kingdom of Heaven, who will?

JANUARY 23

There is no God like the God of Abraham, Isaac, and Jacob. He hears all prayers, and no prior appointments are necessary. Give yourself a gift by sitting in quiet meditation with the King of the universe, the only true and living Lord.

When we heard this, we lost heart, and everyone's courage failed because of you, for the Lord your God is God in heaven above and on earth below.

✡ *Joshua 2:11*

In Yeshua's great instructional prayer, he teaches us to ask that the Father's will be done here on earth, as it is in heaven. As a disciple of Yeshua, you are an important part of God's plan to invade the darkness of this fallen world, and to replace it with the glory of the Kingdom of Heaven. The darkness trembles before the light of God's invasion! Whatever you do today, do it for the Kingdom.

Perhaps begin praying like so: "Dear Lord, please make me a strong soldier in your army. Show me ways in which I might live my life for you. I really need help with…"

<u>JANUARY 24</u>

At the end of a long race it is important to finish well. You may be tired, and you may be exhausted, but the Lord will strengthen you when you are running low. In your quiet time, look back on your days, and consider how you would like to finish.

Therefore, a Sabbath rest remains for God's people. For the person who has entered his rest has rested from his own works, just as God did from his.

✡ *Hebrews 4:9-10*

When God finished his work of creation, he rested, not because he was tired, but because his work was finished. We take a Sabbath rest not because we are finished with all our toil, but because we need the rest. Remember that you are the *creature*, and he is the *Creator*. When you take a much needed rest, it is an acknowledgment of your human limitations. If you do not intentionally take a rest from your work, you will be forced to take one when you break down and fall sick.

Take a deep breath, and pray for the Lord to walk with you, not only throughout your day, but into the great Sabbath rest in the Kingdom of Yeshua.

"Loving Heavenly Father, help me to rest in you and…"

<u>JANUARY 25</u>

A new day presents new opportunities, and fresh ways in which you may encounter the Lord. As you survey the possibilities today may hold, make the choice to carve out *specific times* during each day when you can draw close to the God of all things.

If you fear the Lord, worship and obey him, and if you don't rebel against the Lord's command, then both you and the king who reigns over you will follow the Lord your God.

✡ *1 Samuel 12:14*

Notice the word '*if*' at the very start of this verse. You can imagine a '*but*' would follow afterwards: *If* you follow Yeshua, and *if* the people in authority above you do too, then good! God will smile on you, on your supervisors, and those who are serving under you. *But* if not, then it doesn't matter who is in charge, because the Lord – who is the ruler over all kings and authorities – will not be in support of your endeavors.

Sometimes in life you may even have to stand alone for the Lord, when nobody else does. Are you willing to do that if necessary? You never know what may happen! Best to pray humbly: "Dear Lord, I need help serving and obeying you. Please help me not to sin, but to love you and others by…"

JANUARY 26

Maybe your day has only just begun, and yet you feel like you already want a do-over! Has it been a long winter? Take the time to sit before the Lord, to quiet your heart down, and clear your mind of all the noise. Allow him to speak to you. Your Heavenly Father knows what you need in all aspects of life, and he will meet you personally in your prayer time.

Samuel replied, "Don't be afraid. Even though you have committed all this evil, don't turn away from following the Lord. Instead, worship the Lord with all your heart.

✡ *1 Samuel 12:20*

There are times when each one of us sins. When we do, if we are spiritually sensitive, we will consistently feel *guilty*. It is important to know that guilt can be used by God to correct us when we sin, but God does not *shame* a person who regrets sinning. You may be feeling convicted of something you did or said already today. But as this passage says, yet do not turn away from the Lord, but re-double your efforts to worship him wholeheartedly.

Every child of God is a work-in-progress, and ultimately you are not being judged based on how well you do, but rather on the crosswork of Yeshua. In your prayer time, thank him for his grace today.

JANUARY 27

Are there things which get in the way of your devotion to God? Right now you have a chance to allow the Lord into your heart, to work on your mind, and clear away some of the clutter that gets in the way.

Don't turn away to follow worthless things that can't profit or rescue you; they are worthless.

✡ *1 Samuel 12:21*

An idol in our day is usually not a hand-carved figurine, as in ancient times. Today we have modern idols: Cars, money, gadgets, sex, people, etc. Anything set above God is an idol, and God calls it *worthless*, because it cannot save you into Heaven.

Pray and ask God to rescue you from all forms of idolatry, and to lead you into his Kingdom instead. "Loving Heavenly Father, please show me the idols in my life and help me worship you alone. I sense that I need help with…"

JANUARY 28

God has more to offer you than this world has. He watches our lives, and involves himself with us so intimately that we sometimes forget he is there. Take time to commune directly with your Creator. He sent his son, Yeshua, so that you would have personal access to his throne room.

I am giving you the work of the priesthood as a gift.

✿ *Numbers 18:7b*

As a disciple of Yeshua, you are a very fortunate person. You do not have to go through a temple system, or offer animal sacrifices, but instead you can pray to God directly, and he will hear your prayers, by the power of the Holy Spirit who lives inside you. In that way you are a priest yourself, in a New Covenant sense. You can approach God at any time, with any concern, and tell him anything. That is a *gift* to you!

Take advantage of the great personal relationship you have with Yeshua by praying, "Loving Lord, here is what is on my heart today…"

<u>JANUARY 29</u>

It is best not to hold on to worthless things which can only harm you. After all, we come into the world with nothing, and the only thing we leave with is our soul. Center your focus on Yeshua today, and prepare your heart and mind for what the Lord has for you.

You must present the entire offering due the Lord from all your gifts. The best part of the tenth is to be consecrated.

✡ *Numbers 18:29*

Everything we are given belongs to God, and comes from his hand. Often things may come into our possession in order to test us. Will we be greedy with our prosperity? Will we be responsible? Will we turn otherwise good things into idols? In the case of those things which become idols, will we dispose of them in order to draw closer to God? Even things we love can become idols, and yet everything is seen by the Lord.

To pass the test, allow God to have sovereignty over all your worldly possessions. Worship God with your money, your time, your possessions, and your relationships. Bring him the very best of everything. He knows how to handle it all better than we do, and he will use everything to work together for the good of those who love him. Today begin praying like so: "Dear God, I want to glorify you, and give you everything that I have, starting with..."

JANUARY 30

As the month draws to a close, consider the people in your local fellowship. Go through the ritual of preparing for your heart to worship God, and think about those with whom you share in the community of faith. God has brought you this far, and there are many others on the road with you. Lift them up in prayer before you are finished today.

The Lord will not abandon his people, because of his great name and because he has determined to make you his own people.

✡ *1 Samuel 12:22*

If you are a follower of Yeshua, you are God's own child. He delights in you, even when you don't feel good about yourself. He accepts you entirely, knowing that we all have faults, and that one day, for the sake of his great Name, we will be perfected, standing before him in glory and honor.

Lift your eyes up to the heavens, and give thanks to the Lord. "Dear God, I know you are good! Thank you for *everything*. Thank you for…"

<u>JANUARY 31</u>

It may be that you feel you aren't ready for the new month. Place your trust in the Lord, take some time to center your focus on him, and you will find that he strengthens you from the inside. Start by meditating deeply on his word.

Then the Lord said to Moses, "Make a snake image and mount it on a pole. When anyone who is bitten looks at it, he will recover." So Moses made a bronze snake and mounted it on a pole. Whenever someone was bitten, and he looked at the bronze snake, he recovered.

✡ *Numbers 21:8-9*

Inspired by this story, the widely recognized symbol for *healing* emblazed on the sides of many ambulances is a picture of a snake entwined around a staff.

Consider this: If you were in mortal danger, and all you needed to do was to *look* at a certain sculpture, wouldn't you look at it immediately? Take the time to thank Yeshua for providing a cure for the deadly spiritual poison called sin. "Dear Lord and Savior, *I look to you* for my salvation and rescue today…"

FEBRUARY 1

As your year unfolds, take time to notice the little things which are really not-so-little. The earth belongs to the Lord, and it has been crafted with the finest detail, the most beautiful workmanship. For a few minutes, consider the handiwork of God on a small scale, then allow the wisdom of his word to penetrate even deeper…

This is what the Lord says: Heaven is my throne, and earth is my footstool. Where could you possibly build a house for me? And where would my resting place be?

✡ *Isaiah 66:1*

It is easy to feel small in the larger world. Consider your favorite paths and the places you travel to as you go about your daily routines. In your mind's eye, try to imagine your home – your personal sanctuary – as well as your neighborhood, your city, and then the entire world filled with the glory of God. Then pray that his will would be done on earth, as it is already done in heaven: "Loving Lord…"

FEBRUARY 2

We often think of God as being far off, distant, and remote. But if you have placed your trust in Yeshua, then you can take solace in the fact that God has moved into your heart, and taken up residence in your soul. You will still have many struggles in life, but your ultimate destiny is firmly set, and you are headed to glory.

My hand made all these things, and so they all came into being. This is the Lord's declaration.

✡ *Isaiah 66:2a*

It may be easy to draw a line in the sand, and make judgments between good vs. bad. But the Lord sees all things as either holy, or unholy. He does not judge your skin color, your face, or your body. He only looks at your heart towards him. God made you because he *fore-loved* you, and even though you do not love everything about yourself, he is looking at *what you will be* one day, when you stand in his presence – perfected and completed. He already sees you that way. Determine that you will allow him to do his work in you, and finish the refining process.

You might start your prayers with, "Dear God, by your hand, please make me holy, starting with…"

FEBRUARY 3

Starting your day with the Lord has many benefits. You can step out into the world with the right priorities, a richer understanding, and a hopeful outlook. When you cultivate a disciplined daily devotional time with God, you will find that your life begins to deepen. Also, your appetite for his word will continue to grow.

I will look favorably on this kind of person: one who is humble, submissive in spirit, and trembles at my word.

✡ *Isaiah 66:2*

It is said that in order to teach, one must first be a learner. Who better to learn from than our Maker? When you come to God as one of his pupils – a disciple of Yeshua – he will shape you into the person you always wanted to be, but could never become on your own. It is a life-long process, and it starts with the position of humility, being teachable, and having a healthy sense of awe for the words of God.

Read the verse again, very slowly, taking time to digest each word. Then pray accordingly.

FEBRUARY 4

Before you pray, stop to recall a worship song you love, something you can hum as you go along. You may not feel you have the best singing voice, but God is not listening for pitch or tone. He is listening to your heart. Pick a song that has words that inspire you to worship. Then carry the poetry of those words with you throughout your day.

A sound of uproar from the city! A voice from the temple — the voice of the Lord, paying back his enemies what they deserve!

✡ *Isaiah 66:6*

Often times we long to see injustices set right. The Lord does too! We may wonder why God would allow evil to continue when there are good people being trampled on. His answer is found in the crosswork of Yeshua. At the cross he took full penalty for all the sin which temporarily prevails, and thus defeated the darkness once and for all. There will be a day of great singing and rejoicing, when God determines it is time to bring all his enemies to their final end.

Today, allow your prayers to flow forth with gratitude.

FEBRUARY 5

As your days unfold, stop and re-focus. Take some deep breaths, close your eyes, and allow Yeshua to fill your thoughts. If it has been busy, let him carry your burden. Give him your worries and cares. You are not alone, and there is a great reward for your waiting in heaven. Also, you can take comfort in your friends, who were put in your life as a blessing from God.

Once you were not a people, but now you are God's people; you had not received mercy, but now you have received mercy.

✡ *1 Peter 2:10*

When you honestly look back on your day, your week, your life, you will find that you have some regrets. Isn't it good that God has shown mercy to those of us who are far less than perfect? Those of us who look to Yeshua are united in our desperate need for mercy. And by his grace, he is willing to be merciful toward us. Allow him to build your confidence. You serve a great God, and what he has done for you cannot ever be erased. Tell him what is on your mind tofay!

"Dear Heavenly Father…"

FEBRUARY 6

It is a new day! Have life's worries kept you down?
Have you been feeling overwhelmed? Take it all to
Yeshua. A good understanding of his crosswork
will change your perspective, and your entire life.

*Jesus answered, "Destroy this temple, and I will
raise it up in three days." Therefore the Jews said,
"This temple took forty-six years to build, and will
you raise it up in three days?" But he was speaking
about the temple of his body.*

✡ *John 2:19-21*

After being crucified, Yeshua died and was buried.
There was no question he was dead. (People back
in ancient times knew quite well what *dead* looked
like.) But three days later he resurrected himself
from the grave. That is a testimony to the awesome
might of our risen Savior. Yeshua truly *is* both
Lord and God!

Take some time and allow the reality of his
resurrection to penetrate your thoughts and prayers.
When you are ready, begin by praying, "Dear Lord,
I want to experience your resurrection in my life
too…"

FEBRUARY 7

A 'disciple' is someone who follows the *discipline* of his or her teacher. If you follow Yeshua, you will become ever more like your teacher as time goes by, until one day you will be raised from the dead yourself!

So when he was raised from the dead, his disciples remembered that he had said this, and they believed the Scripture and the statement Jesus had made.

✡ *John 2:22*

Even those people who were his very earliest disciples were not able to fully believe in Yeshua until after his resurrection. Only then were they able to understand the Hebrew Scriptures with 20/20 hindsight. Remember, they did not have the Greek Scriptures at first. They simply had the Torah, the Prophets, and the Writings.

Today there are lots of people who study the Bible, yet do not truly believe in the risen Messiah. But take heart! You do not need to be a scholar or theologian be a disciple of the Lord, Yeshua. You need only invite him into your heart.

Pray as follows, then continue on your own: "Loving Heavenly Father, teach me more about your ways…"

FEBRUARY 8

Take a few moments and rest in the Lord's presence. Close your eyes, and take a deep breath. When you sense his peace, read over the following verse…

While he was in Jerusalem during the Passover Festival, many believed in his name when they saw the signs he was doing.

✡ *John 2:23-24*

One of the reasons so many people dismiss the Bible is because they assume miracles cannot happen. People in Yeshua's time were able to see him perform signs and miracles, and so they believed in his name, but what about those of us who came much later?

In truth, a miracle does not need to be flashy, or spectacular, in order to come from the hand of God. If you have ever had a small miracle occur in your life, you can thank the Lord for his grace and mercy. He will provide everything you need, and sometimes you will sense his miraculous presence in the most ordinary of circumstances.

FEBRUARY 9

Get ready for a new day by clearing all the clutter from your thoughts, and focusing only on the Lord Yeshua. Take several minutes if you need to. Ask him to settle your emotions, and meet you in your devotional time. He is always there, eager to share time with you.

"Jesus, however, would not entrust himself to them, since he knew them all..."

✡ *John 2:24*

It is very easy to look out at the world, to watch the news, to see what is happening, and become disheartened. Yeshua himself understood that even those same people who followed him were part of the massive mob of humanity, which is driven by a wicked spirit. Because of this, he wisely guarded his own heart. As a human being you too are made in the image of God, and if you follow Yeshua there is something sacred inside of you – the Holy Spirit. It is important, therefore, for you to guard your heart like Yeshua did, and protect your faith. The world will try to rob you of what is most precious, but Yeshua will never let you go, and he has something far greater for you, than what this world has to offer.

Go to him in prayer now. Tell him all your cares.

<u>FEBRUARY 10</u>

Our Lord is good, and you can trust him to be gentle in leading you. You may think you have secrets from him, but he is working deep inside you, to make you holy and clean. Do not be afraid to approach Yeshua for mercy. He is happy to receive you. Read this verse very carefully, and ponder its meaning…

"…he did not need anyone to testify about man; for he himself knew what was in man."

✡ *John 2:25*

Although we are ordinary human beings, just like everybody else, each of us has been uniquely endowed with character traits and a personality which is all our own. God knows this, because he put you together in just such a way. And although Yeshua had to wisely guard his heart from the mass of humanity, he also knew what was inside each person.

The Lord can look upon an individual heart and know what its deepest thoughts are. In light of this, aren't you glad the Lord is kind and merciful? Pray today that the Lord would give you a clean heart, and pure motives.

"Dear Lord, I know you can see the state of my heart, and my motives. I love you, I thank you, and I confess…"

FEBRUARY 11

Looking back on your most recent days, do not be too hard on yourself if you feel like you have not done everything you could have. When you place your trust in Yeshua, the Lord does not look at you with an eye towards punishment. Rather, he sees you as a parent sees a beloved child, just learning how to crawl, and struggling along the way. If you have trusted him, that is all he asks of you.

Mankind, he has told each of you what is good and what it is the Lord requires of you: to act justly, to love faithfulness, and to walk humbly with your God.

✡ *Micah 6:8*

This is one of the most important, yet least known, verses in the Hebrew Scriptures. For an enlightening read, open your Bible and study the entire chapter. You will find that God is far less interested in religious ritual than he is with the moral state of your heart. Make this verse your prayer for today.

"Dear God, help me to act justly, to love faithfulness, and to walk humbly with you today. I need you to help me with…"

<u>FEBRUARY 12</u>

Calm your heart, close your eyes, breathe deeply, and invite the Lord into your devotional time. Begin the day with Yeshua, and ask him to be your guide, your king, and your friend. When you step out into the world you will be secure in the knowledge that God is with you. Read and re-read this important verse…

"I chose you before I formed you in the womb."

✡ *Jeremiah 1:5a*

Have you ever considered the notion that God has people in mind before conception and birth? His thoughts are much higher than ours, but isn't it intriguing to imagine what sort of creativity the Lord uses to dream up individual human beings?

Made in God's image, people are both priceless and sacred. Psalm 8 tells us that people are just "a little lower than the angels." Thank God he has stamped his image upon you!

Take time today to ponder the wonder of being created in his image, then express your appreciate to him in prayer. He knew you before you knew yourself!

FEBRUARY 13

When you come to God with your worries and cares, he is there to receive you. There is nothing you can tell him that will frighten, scandalize, or surprise him. Maybe you have thought of God as a distant watcher, someone who is cold and far away, waiting for you to sin so that he can harm you. Nothing could be further from the truth. The Lord wants to come alongside you, help you through life, and usher you into his heavenly kingdom.

But I protested, "Oh no, Lord God! Look, I don't know how to speak since I am only a youth."

✡ *Jeremiah 1:6*

Jeremiah was sent by God to indict his own people of sin – an awful calling! He was quick to point out to God that, unfortunately, he would not be able to speak well enough to handle the job. But God can use people to do many things they themselves never imagined they could do.

As you meditate on this verse, stop and consider some of the things in your life which you feel are beyond your ability. If God commanded you to go forth and do those very things, would you trust that he would see you through? In prayer, ask God to clearly show you some areas in where you could use some growth, by stepping out of your comfort zone.

FEBRUARY 14

As you center your focus on the Lord, ask him to make you sensitive to his divine leading, and to his call on your life. Sometimes it may be difficult to know exactly what to do, but when you open your heart to Yeshua each day, you can trust him to show you the right path.

Then the Lord said to me: Do not say, "I am only a youth," for you will go to everyone I send you to and speak whatever I tell you.

✡ *Jeremiah 1:7*

It is not always easy to discern the specific direction to which God is calling us in the daily life, and sometimes we are faced with choices that can feel like big risks. But if you trust in Yeshua, he will guide you along, like a river flowing over the stones, moving you in the righteous path – toward heaven.

Pray today, "Loving Lord, please allow my actions to reflect your will. Make me more like you in the following ways…"

FEBRUARY 15

Another day ahead of you, another behind. As your life unfolds how do you conduct yourself? Do you see yourself growing in faith, or do you see yourself barely holding on? If you are like most of us, it's something of a mix: The longer you live, the more you see how much you need God. Come to him today in humility. He loves you!

Do not be afraid of anyone, for I will be with you to rescue you. This is the Lord's declaration.

✡ *Jeremiah 1:8*

It has been said, if God told you to run and drive your head straight into a brick wall, the wisest thing you could do would be to obey, trusting him to put a hole in the right place just in the nick of time! God called Jeremiah to say specific things to certain people who would not have been at all happy to hear his message. But God was on his side.

When God is with you, why be afraid of people? If Yeshua is in your heart, you can rest easy, knowing he will send you to the right places and rescue you from evil. In prayer today, ask him: "Loving Lord, please blaze the trail today. Lead me in your ways. I trust you for…"

FEBRUARY 16

Today you have a fresh opportunity to live for
Yeshua. Make the most of it! You have been given
a gift, and the time you spend living for the glory of
Lamb of God is not wasted time. So before you
step out, devote some quiet time to your Savior.
There is nobody else in the world who can help you
like he can. You will be grateful you for his
company.

Consider this challenging verse…

*"I will pronounce my judgments against them for
all the evil they did when they abandoned me."*

✡ *Jeremiah 1:16a*

Every honest person knows that he / she has sinned.
The important thing is confessing it to Yeshua.
Sometimes we have to learn hard lessons in life, and
when we do, it can seem like God is out to punish
us. If you have ever felt convicted in your heart
because of something you have done, know this:
God often uses difficult times to change our
thoughts, attitudes, and actions.

Every sinner should be thankful that God is loving
enough to reveal his clear moral judgment. It is
through his crosswork, and his corrective rod, that
he removes sin from the lives of those he loves. Go
to him today in prayer over these things.

FEBRUARY 17

Settle in for some time with your God. Look back on your week and consider the ways in which he has directed you.

As your devotional time begins, ask him to help you take stock in a spiritual way. Ask Yeshua: Have my priorities been in line? Have I taken advantage of opportunities presented to me? Thankfully, God is in the business of helping us to grow through grace, and there is nothing he cannot do.

"Now, get ready. Stand up and tell them everything that I command you. Do not be intimidated by them or I will cause you to cower before them."

✡ *Jeremiah 1:17*

When it comes time to choose sides in this life, *always* choose to be on God's side. He is doing a mighty work in this world, and inside of you, which will have eternal consequences. Make sure to surrender everything to him, and ask him to help you worship in spirit and in truth.

Start today by praying something like this: "Almighty God, I need you more than ever, and I want to stand firmly on your side. Help me to do that today by..."

FEBRUARY 18

Sometimes life gets the better of us. We do the best we can, and we work hard, but in the end our feet are made of clay. We are all sinners. That is why a wise person will come to God each and every day, asking for help and discernment. As you prepare for another adventure, take time to invite the Lord into your place of prayer, to direct your growth. The apostle James has some bold insights for us...

What is the source of wars and fights among you? Don't they come from your passions that wage war within you?

✡ *James 4:1*

If you have lived very long at all, you will no doubt experience friction on a regular basis. Sometimes even in your own faith community. It is tragic when believers allow rifts to develop between one another. Rifts can easily turn into deep division, and sometimes hostility. But that is not what Yeshua has called us too. We are to be agents of healing, by his grace.

Bring all this to the Lord today. Ask him to aim his searchlight directly into your own heart, and to sanctify your perspective towards other people.

"Dear God, you know how much trouble I've had, so I need help with..."

FEBRUARY 19

Over time, your prayer life can enrich everything you do. If you cultivate a regular devotional time, you will find yourself feeling empty on days when you skip it. But your Heavenly Father is always there to minister to you, and to give you his Spirit. Breathe in, and slowly breathe out. Take several moments to be still before Yeshua. Remember what he has done for you. When you are settled, consider this verse from James.

You ask and don't receive because you ask with wrong motives, so that you may spend it on your pleasures.

✡ *James 4:3*

It is too easy to conclude that, if you ask God for something, and use the right 'prayer formula' then he will give you whatever you want. That is hardly ever the case, and that is not the nature of the faith walk. *True faith* trusts the wisdom of God. It does not simply lay claim to material possessions. Far more importantly, God is highly concerned with our internal motives.

If you have not done so lately, today, rather than asking God to meet only your material needs, ask him to purify your heart's motives!

FEBRUARY 20

God is *holy*. Completely, and entirely *holy*. Have you ever stopped to consider that impact of that word? If you are in Yeshua, you are already holy, and set apart. He is your friend. Set your heart on him today in prayer and gratitude.

So whoever wants to be the friend of the world becomes the enemy of God.

✡ *James 4:4*

Yeshua died and rose again to set you free. But biblical freedom is not the same as 'freedom of choice.' Biblical freedom is the freedom to live *as a child of God* with nothing keeping you from growing in him, more each day.

In Yeshua, you are free to *be a true friend of God*, released from the bondage of sin!

"Dear Lord, please be my friend, and make me yours…"

FEBRUARY 21

Sometimes you may feel like your devotion to God is not 'paying off.' If you have tried to be humble, prayerful, and gentle, but still people step on you, take heart: You are in good company. Yeshua was kicked, bruised, and beaten. If you are tempted to take matters into your own hands, stop. Today is a new day, and you have a fresh opportunity to give your life over to him. He will lead you in the very best way.

But he gives greater grace. Therefore he says: God resists the proud, but gives grace to the humble.

✡ *James 4:6*

It is not easy to rank yourself lower than others. Everything in us wants to stand up and say, "But I have rights!" To be humble before God means allowing him to fight on your behalf.

If you are a friend of God – and not in love with this fallen world – then he will *teach you through grace*. Isn't that how you would rather learn life's lessons? (By grace?) Pray for that sort of education today!

You might begin with, "Loving Lord, please teach me humility. I do not want to learn things the hard way, so I ask you to teach me with grace..."

<u>FEBRUARY 22</u>

In all the struggles of daily life we sometimes forget there exists a spiritual world, where angels and demons rage, and where *things unseen* contest for the souls of men and women. Put on the armor of God today! In your prayer time, ask the Lord to prepare you for this day, and also for the long road ahead. He is not finished with you yet!

Therefore, submit to God. Resist the devil, and he will flee from you.

✡ *James 4:7*

This verse calls us to *submit*, and to *resist*. Submit to God, and resist the devil. Often times a zealous person will try to "bind" the devil, but the Bible never instructs us to bind.

We are called to *submit* to God, who fights our battles, and in doing so, to *resist* not only the evil spirit that governs this world, but also the evil that wells up in our own hearts. Remember what James taught earlier in the same chapter: *What causes fights and quarrels? Your desires that battle within you!*

In the great invisible spiritual war, the real battlefield is deep inside the human heart. Take the time then, to give your heart to Yeshua in a fresh way. He has sealed you for the day of redemption, and he will fill you with wisdom and the Holy Spirit. Pray, "Loving Heavenly Father, I *submit* to you today in the following areas…"

FEBRUARY 23

Two of the most important keys to understanding
Scripture, are *mystery* and *paradox*. Mystery –
because we cannot grasp the ways of God. And
paradox – because many things which seem to be
entirely contradictory are reconciled in Yeshua.
Consider mystery and paradox in this passage from
James, then pray using his words as a guide…

*Draw near to God, and he will draw near to you.
Cleanse your hands, sinners, and purify your
hearts, you double-minded. Be miserable and
mourn and weep. Let your laughter be turned to
mourning and your joy to gloom. Humble
yourselves before the Lord, and he will exalt you.*

✡ *James 4:7-10*

How can our grief and mourning become laughter?
How can humility result in elevation? Only in
Yeshua are these things possible. He turns
everything right-side up.

Here's how: If you are weak, allow yourself to be
weak in him. If you are miserable, be miserable in
him. That is the honest thing to do. God knows
what's *really* happening with you, so why hide it
from him? If you are honest with God he will take
care of the rest.

FEBRUARY 24

Before you begin another rough and tumble day, make sure to refill your spirit with the living word of God. The Lord makes all things new, and as you look to the future, commit yourself to a life well-lived. You don't need to be rich or powerful to have a relationship with the Creator of the universe.

Across the Jordan in the land of Moab, Moses began to explain this law, saying: "The Lord our God spoke to us at Horeb: You have stayed at this mountain long enough."

✡ *Deuteronomy 1:5-6*

In reading any section of the Bible, it is important to consider whose voice is speaking. In Deuteronomy we hear the voice of Moses, preaching to the children of Israel on God's behalf. You have probably heard many preachers speaking, but if you ever want to listen to Moses preaching, pick up Deuteronomy.

In this opening verse, Moses begins to preach by telling the people that they have *"stayed at this mountain long enough!"* It's time to move on!

Are there certain places in your life where the Lord has indicated that you have stayed long enough? Maybe it's time to let some things go, and move on. Pray and ask God for wisdom, as you step out in faith today, move toward the future God has for you.

FEBRUARY 25

Growing in Yeshua is something we cooperate with. The Lord calls us to abide in him, as he sustains us and nourishes us with loving care. Take some time to allow God to open your heart and mind to his word. Then consider what Isaiah says…

Listen, heavens, and pay attention, earth, for the Lord has spoken: I have raised children and brought them up, but they have rebelled against me.

✡ *Isaiah 1:2*

If you have ever opened up the prophets and felt confused, perhaps it is because it seems sometimes as if there are lots of different voices speaking. As we have seen, it is always important to consider whose *voice* is being heard. In the case of Isaiah, and the prophets, the Lord often speaks in a courtroom setting.

Re-read this verse and imagine a lawyer making his opening arguments. The voice of the Lord is heard as the judge, the jury, and the attorney, all within the courtroom of heaven. If you read the prophets with this idea in mind, much will become clear.

Be thankful that God is a merciful judge, who has achieved his divine justice through the crosswork of Yeshua!

FEBRUARY 26

God cares deeply about those who have very little. Remember: The Lord writes the law, judges sin, and executes justice. Take time today to recount the goodness he has brought to you, and pray to him with a humble heart.

We return again to the courtroom…

Learn to do what is good. Pursue justice. Correct the oppressor. Defend the rights of the fatherless. Plead the widow's cause.

✡ *Isaiah 1:17*

In the law courtroom of God, we are encouraged by the Lord to "plead the case" of those who are vulnerable. He charges us to learn to do right, and seek justice, following his holy example.

So in the same way the Lord holds court in heaven, we are called to fight for good in this world, in whatever sphere of life we travel in.

Ask him how you might you do your part today!

FEBRUARY 27

We can turn to the Lord in our times of deepest
need. If you have ever felt like you have done
something to be disqualified from God's mercy,
perish the thought! That is the best time to come to
Yeshua. Do not allow yourself to feel like you
cannot approach God, or participate in the Lord's
supper. Our God is a merciful judge, and a loving
Father.

*"Come, let us settle this," says the Lord. "Though
your sins are scarlet, they will be as white as snow;
though they are crimson red, they will be like
wool."*

✡ *Isaiah 1:18*

Imagine again a lawyer giving his closing
arguments in court. *"Let us settle the matter,"* the
Lord says. God sees all your sins and faults, brings
you before the courts of heaven, and states his case:
You have been found guilty of sin! The testimony
is enough to convict you. But as a follower of
Yeshua, you are seen not there before him as a mere
defendant, but as a *child of God.*

"Let us settle this," he says. Your sins will be
completely washed away, and you will stand clean
before your Loving Heavenly Father, thanks to the
grace of Yeshua.

Pray to him today, "Dear Lord, I am grateful for
your shalom, and your grace, and your mercy. I
praise you because you..."

FEBRUARY 28

Allow yourself to relax as you enter into fellowship with God. You are safe with him. The Lord of all creation has time for you. Come to him with all your worries and let him carry your burden.

Consider this tricky verse…

I will turn my hand against you and will burn away your dross completely; I will remove all your impurities.

✡ *Isaiah 1:25*

An amazing thing happens in the law court of God: Perfect justice is executed. You might be tempted to think that divine justice simply spells punishment, but for those who trust in Yeshua, his justice is both *purging* and *purifying*.

Read this verse again several times, and allow your understanding to change. The final Judgment Day will bring a glorious transformation for those of us who struggle with sin, but trust in Yeshua.

In your prayers today, make sure to spend some time expressing your love to God. Thanks to Yeshua, he sees you as his child, no longer an enemy.

MARCH 1

The Bible speaks of "meditating" on God's word. In our modern vernacular, *meditation* means *emptying* your mind of all thoughts. But biblical meditation means *filling* your thoughts with the word of God. Take time then to meditate on this verse today, and ponder it deeply…

While they were stoning Stephen, he called out: "Lord Jesus, receive my spirit!"

✡ *Acts 7:59*

When a crisis hits, where do you turn? Does it take long for you to call out to God in times of trouble, when you are suddenly shaken? Or do you reflexively turn to Yeshua.

Over time your habitual cultivation of spiritual discipline will result in the same response Stephen had. During his life's worst moment, he is in prayer. Isn't that how you'd like to be? God's word shapes us so that we learn to live well, to walk upright, to fight for good, to protect the innocent, and finally to die well.

He is your friend. Be with him today.

MARCH 2

This next several devotionals will focus on the greatest command – to *love*. On the heels of the Shema, that timeless cry of Judaism, comes the following famous verse…

Love the Lord your God with all your heart, with all your soul, and with all your strength.

✡ *Deuteronomy 6:5*

When asked, Yeshua told an expert in the law that this was The Greatest Command. Moreover, he said, the second was similar: "*Love* your neighbor as yourself." Yeshua even went as far as to say, "All the Law and the Prophets hang on these two commands!" (Matt. 22:34-40)

Love is an action, as well as a mindset. In your prayer time today, ask the Lord to guide you toward a deeper understanding of what it means to *love*. God is love, but love is not a god.

Loving takes commitment, and at times personal sacrifice for others. Pray for wisdom, that God might show you how to see the Law through the lens of *love*. Start by praying, "Loving Lord, I want to understand how your *love* is expressed. Please quicken my heart and open my mind to your way of seeing things. I ask you today to help me *love* you and other people by…"

MARCH 3

Looking at the Law through the lens of love, means understanding that loving God and humanity calls for *positive action*. Loving is *an activity*. It is alive, and vigorous. When you love, you *do* something. (Loving God and your neighbor is not about avoiding action.)

We will look at some of the 10 Commandments through the lens of love, and see how the negative prohibitions – *thou shalt not* – may be understood as positive actions *to love*.

"Do not murder."

✡ *Deuteronomy 5:17*

It is easy for one to think, "Well, I'm not a murderer, so I'm not that bad!" But Yeshua taught clearly that *hatred* in the human heart is akin to murder! Moreover, if we were to look at this prohibition through the *lens of love*, we see that it is not enough to simply avoid murder and hatred. We must also love! Love means action. So what does the prohibition "*You shall not murder*" become, when turned into a positive commandment to love?

Quite simply, it becomes, "*You shall protect life.*"

Pray today: "Lord, how might I love in this way? How might I show the love of Yeshua by protecting life?"

MARCH 4

In your prayer time today, as always, take several moments to allow the Lord to fill you with his Holy Spirit. God is guiding you with his love and wisdom. Invite Yeshua into your devotional time, and pray for his peace to fill you today, and prepare your heart.

"Do not commit adultery."

✡ *Deuteronomy 5:18*

In the same manner as we have seen, how might this prohibition take shape in your life, if you were to see it through the positive command to love?

It is not enough to avoid adultery and lust! In order to act in love, we must also sanctify marriage. That is what this prohibition becomes when seen through the lens of love: You *shall* protect marriage. Take this to Yeshua today!

__MARCH 5__

Taking time to come before the Lord every day is extremely healthy, and it is not a selfish thing to do. When you come to him in prayer, you make yourself more available to be used by him for other people. Relax your thoughts, sit quietly, close your eyes, and take a few breaths. Yeshua is with you wherever you go. He will never leave you nor forsake you. And his mercies are new every morning.

"Do not steal."

✡ *Deuteronomy 5:19*

Looking at this command through the lens of love, "You shall *not* steal," becomes "You *shall* protect other people's property!"

God gives certain gifts and items to people for their well-being and protection, but greed causes people to violate this command. If you are to step out in *love* today, *as The Greatest Commandment* calls us to do, you must be willing to help protect other people from theft. But if you have never thought of the law in this way before, ask God to help you grow. He will!

You might pray, "Dear Lord, I have always thought it was good enough to avoid stealing, but please help me to step out and become a protector of other people by loving them in the following ways…"

MARCH 6

Sometimes it feels like this dirty fallen world has just attached itself to you, and it won't let you go. But you can be washed in the water of the word, and the blood of Yeshua! He has overcome this world, and claimed victory on your behalf. Isn't that a great reason to rejoice today? Before you charge out the door, take some time to worship the Lord in your heart. Come to him with trust and open hands. He loves you greatly!

"Do not give dishonest testimony against your neighbor."

✡ *Deuteronomy 5:20*

This commandment shows us that part of God's personality is that he views *truth* as sacred.

Have you ever felt violated by lies? If so, you know why God hates false testimony. It hurts people and harms their credibility. But the Greatest Commandment calls us to *love*, and no child of God is ever meant to become a character assassin. Rather, we are to see *truth* the same way God sees it – as holy, and important to protect.

Pray today that God would make you into a protector of truth. Consider practical ways in which you might love God and mankind, by standing up for what is true. "Loving Heavenly Father, please make my heart true today, like yours. Put me on the true path as I..."

MARCH 7

As your days roll on, give thanks to God for all he has done, and ask him to teach you by his grace. You have Yeshua, so you have everything.

"Do not covet your neighbor's wife or desire your neighbor's house, his field, his male or female slave, his ox or donkey, or anything that belongs to your neighbor."

✡ Deuteronomy 5:21

Covetousness is the root cause of so many sins. It is a misguided desire of the heart. Covetousness leads people to steal, to kill, to lie, and to violate other people and their possessions.

By now you know that God calls us to *love* instead. How might you counter covetousness in your own heart and in the world around you, with love? Use the *lens of love* in prayer..._

<u>MARCH 8</u>

When you open your eyes in the morning, do you take the time to direct your thoughts toward the Lord? Take some time now, close your eyes, and listen to the sound of your own heartbeat. What (or Who!) keeps it beating? This week ask God to increase your trust in his plan for your life. Ask him to strengthen your faith.

By faith Abraham, when he was called, obeyed and set out for a place that he was going to receive as an inheritance. He went out, even though he did not know where he was going.

✡ *Hebrews 11:8*

In a very real sense, none of us knows exactly where we are going. Every person will pass through this life, and step into an eternal state, but what that "place" will look like is anybody's guess. Walking by faith means actively trusting God to direct your path towards *himself.*

In Yeshua your inheritance is like Abraham's Promised Land – a place to where God is ultimately calling you. He is your inheritance, and your destination, and your promised land.

Start praying today, "Dear Heavenly Father, please make me more aware of your encroaching kingdom all around me, as I walk by faith. Help me as I…"

MARCH 9

This world is fallen, and hostile. But we are called to walk by faith through the trials and tears of life. No one ever said it would be easy! But you can take great comfort in the fact that God has reconciled you to himself in Yeshua, and that he has paved the way for your arrival in his kingdom.

By faith he stayed as a foreigner in the land of promise, living in tents as did Isaac and Jacob, coheirs of the same promise.

✡ *Hebrews 11:9*

An 'heir' is one who stands to gain from the generosity of a relative who passes away. In Yeshua, you have a relative who has died, and left you something priceless. Along with Abraham, Isaac, and Jacob – the patriarchs of Judaism – you have a home in the Promised Land, the kingdom of God, thanks to the resurrected Lord.

For right now, you live in a temporary dwelling, like a tent, in a land that is not your true home. But someday the promise of God will be fulfilled in your life.

Take time now to be still before the Lord, and meditate on your own connection with Abraham, Isaac, and Jacob – your fellow heirs of the same promise you also have.

MARCH 10

Today is a new day, with fresh chances to enter into fellowship with Yeshua. His life, death, and resurrection provide for you a direct line to the heart of the Father. Like Abraham before you, you are a pilgrim travelling through this world in search of God's righteous path. Allow him to direct you in prayer today.

For he was looking forward to the city that has foundations, whose architect and builder is God.

✡ *Hebrews 11:10*

The heavenly city which God is preparing, is not simply a place with streets of gold. It is also a *people*, who will shine like the stars in the heavens.

Praise God for his goodness today. Recognize the fact that, as a follower of Yeshua, you are already a part of the heavenly city.

MARCH 11

It is not hard to come to God. You need only breathe a sigh of a prayer, and he is right there with you. He attends to your every breath, and he walks with you through every door you enter. Your life is a gift from him, and he loves you. Take some time to allow the Lord to quiet your heart, and focus your thoughts on his faithfulness…

By faith even Sarah herself, when she was unable to have children, received power to conceive offspring, even though she was past the age, since she considered that the one who had promised was faithful.

✡ *Hebrews 11:11*

In ancient Middle Eastern culture, to have children was a blessing, but to be barren was seen as a curse. Sarah was not cursed, she was simply unable to have children without assistance from the Lord.

Is there anything which God has done for you, which you did not think would ever happen in your life? Think back, and recall how grateful you were, and renew your heart for the Lord. He has done great things!

You might begin your prayers with, "Loving Lord, I remember and will never forget the time when you…"

MARCH 12

Prior to 1609, and the invention and use of the telescope by Galileo, it was thought by many that the number of stars in the heavens were finite and easily calculable. This mistaken perspective lead people to believe that Abraham's offspring would be just as easy to calculate. It was not until later – when telescopes became more common – that people understood clearly that Abraham's descendants would be entirely impossible to count...

Therefore, from one man — in fact, from one as good as dead — came offspring as numerous as the stars of the sky and as innumerable as the grains of sand along the seashore.

✡ *Hebrews 11:12*

It is miraculous to consider, but the reality is God can take something dead and bring new life, as he has with Abraham and Sarah. Often times we would like God to bring back something which we have lost, or broken. But new life is not the same as old life.

When a caterpillar transforms into a butterfly, it becomes a very different creature, with a completely different anatomy. If you walk by faith, trusting in Yeshua, then you are one of Abraham's true descendants. Someday you will be completely transformed. New life will come from what was dead. Today, ask God to increase your faith.

MARCH 13

There is a sad trend in the world today, which sees Christians claiming material blessings, and assuming that God's will dictates that they should be rich and healthy at all times. Some go so far as to say poor people, and people who struggle with illnesses lack faith. But Hebrews 11, that great chapter on faith, teaches the exact opposite…

These all died in faith, although they had not received the things that were promised. But they saw them from a distance, greeted them, and confessed that they were foreigners and temporary residents on the earth.

✡ *Hebrews 11:13*

If there are things in this life which you want but cannot have, do not despair. If you are fighting illness, don't lose faith. This life was never meant to be easy, and God does not despise our weakness.

If you had everything you ever wanted, you might be tempted to trust in those material things! Remember who keeps your heart beating. That is a gift in itself.

Pray, "Dear God, help me trust you for the things I need. You know what is best for me. Please help me today as I…"

<u>MARCH 14</u>

We all need to come to the Source, and refill our spirits, in order to step out into the world with a sense of hope and meaning. Your life is significant, never forget! When you take the time to connect with Yeshua in prayer, you align yourself with the awesome plans of God. Be encouraged! He is ready to receive you, and go into the world with you.

On the last and most important day of the festival, Jesus stood up and cried out, "If anyone is thirsty, let him come to me and drink. The one who believes in me, as the Scripture has said, will have streams of living water flow from deep within him."

✡ *John 7:37-38*

It is hard to overstate the importance of water in the desert. When there is a drought, life slows to a painful crawl. But in this passage we see Yeshua announcing in the midst of a celebration: *Trust in me! I will quench your thirst to live!*

Pray today that God would fill your whole person, so that the Messiah would come gushing out of you like a river.

"Loving Lord, in a dry and weary land, I need you. Please refresh me today as I…"

MARCH 15

During the faith-walk, there are times when we must learn to see with spiritual eyes. It is all too easy to get caught up in the concrete world, forgetting that there is a heavenly realm, where the Lord is preparing a place for you. Before you read the following verse, slow things down. Take a breath, close your eyes, and ask God to allow you to see with the eyes of your heart.

He said this about the Spirit. Those who believed in Jesus were going to receive the Spirit, for the Spirit had not yet been given because Jesus had not yet been glorified.

✡ *John 7:39*

Back in days of old the Spirit was given, but could also be taken away, depending on the actions and heart of the individual. But now we trust in the actions of Yeshua, whose perfect sacrifice on the cross allows everyone to approach the living Lord on equal footing. That's something to thank God for!

Start your prayers with, "Dear Yeshua, be glorified in me…"

<u>MARCH 16</u>

Shalom! Another new day, and you are fortunate to know Yeshua. He is your joy and delight. He gives you good things, and protects you from evil. When everyone else has left you hanging, he will *never* forsake you. He is your friend and brother, always interceding for you, always looking out for you. And since he conquered death, paving the path for you to follow in his footsteps, your future is a brighter than you can imagine.

You will indeed go out with joy and be peacefully guided; the mountains and the hills will break into singing before you, and all the trees of the field will clap their hands.

✡ *Isaiah 55:12*

May the God of all peace give you shalom today, as you live your life before him. May he walk with you and guide your steps. May he give you wisdom, courage, and a pure heart. May he bless whatever you set your hand to, and be a light to your vision. All of heaven celebrates when one sinner repents, and you, having come to Yeshua, are a part of that great celebration.

As you prepare for the day, meditate on these things. You might begin your prayer the following way: "Thank you, God. Today I praise you for the way you…"

MARCH 17

If your spirit is tired, when the weight of life is pressing you down, give yourself the gift of spending time with Yeshua. If you have experienced a great loss, bring him the broken pieces and ask him to repair the damage. He is the One who will give you hope, and never let you down.

"Come, everyone who is thirsty, come to the water; and you without silver, come, buy, and eat!"

✡ *Isaiah 55:1*

Here in Isaiah we see the same symbolism Yeshua used in John 7 – water! If you are thirsty, and have no money, the Lord will nourish you for free. Ponder that! It is actually better to die of thirst in the desert and have Yeshua in your heart, than to be a wealthy person who spurns God. His gift to you is priceless, and yet he offers it *free of charge!*

Pray to him today, and ask him to feed your spiritual appetite. "Loving Lord, I hunger and thirst for…"

MARCH 18

After walking with the Lord for some time, you will find that your *tastes* change. Some of the things you used to love are not so attractive anymore, and the people you used to think were strange – followers of Yeshua – are now your dearest friends. Imagine that!

Pay attention and come to me; listen, so that you will live.

✡ *Isaiah 55:3*

If you can see with spiritual eyes, you can also *hear* and *listen* with spiritual ears, finely attuned to God's good promptings. The more you saturate your life with Scripture, the better you will be able to discern the will of God in your daily life.

The Lord has all the range of personality and emotion that any person has, and more – after all, people are made in *his* image! So when you make important decisions, be sure to pray for wisdom, and also give consideration to God's own personal *tastes*. God has *preferences*. One of them is that you would listen to him, and live!

In your prayer time today, you might start by being silent for a period of time, just *listening*.

MARCH 19

Our God is a loving God. He sees you in your struggles and understands what you are going through. He does not look down on you like some insecure person who needs to feel better about himself. No. Rather, he gazes at you with the love of a parent for his child. But unlike our human parents, he is a perfectly merciful Father. There is nothing you could ever do to erase his love for you, through Yeshua. Rest easy in his presence, and carefully consider this uplifting messianic verse…

I will make a permanent covenant with you on the basis of the faithful kindnesses of David.

✡ *Isaiah 55:3*

God's commitment to you is absolutely unshakable and permanent. He brought you out of the mire of sin, and he is determined to get you through this life, arriving before his throne in bright radiance. That is his promise to you.

He gives you his faithful love, *his shalom*, which lifts you out of the dreadful human condition, and sets you alongside people like King David. So you are a part of a huge family! In your individual quiet time, thank God for his everlasting covenant, which puts you on the high road to a great destination with so many others.

Start by praying, "Dear Lord, I long for your kindness…!"

MARCH 20

When you open your eyes in the morning, be sure to open your heart and mind to what the Lord has for you today. God can use the most humdrum details of daily life to call your attention to him. Be thankful, pray, and when circumstances line up against you, be brave and rely on the power of Yeshua.

I — I am the one who comforts you. Who are you that you should fear humans who die, or a son of man who is given up like grass?

✡ *Isaiah 51:12*

This verse puts it all in perspective. The Lord gives you comfort, peace, rest, purpose, life, nourishment, on and on. In Yeshua you have the assurance of eternal life with God – what can mankind take away from someone like you?

Your reward is in heaven, and cannot be cut down like mere grass. Pray today, "Loving God, at times I am afraid. Please help me with this, and help me to trust you today for…"

<u>MARCH 21</u>

There is a place being prepared for you in the heavenly kingdom of Christ Yeshua. For today, prepare a place for your prayers and devotional time. Make yourself comfortable, and go there as consistently as possible. You may even keep a journal nearby, to record your prayers.

The prisoner is soon to be set free; he will not die and go to the Pit, and his food will not be lacking.

✡ *Isaiah 51:14*

A person can be locked away, or restricted in some other way, and still have the freedom of Yeshua inside. Galatians 5:1 tells us that Yeshua has set us free *for the sake of freedom itself!* He lead the children of Israel out of slavery to set them free, and one day there will be a second Exodus, when all those who live in Yeshua will finally be freed from sin and death.

If you have felt chained down by sin, never fear! God will not allow you to die in the dungeon. Cry out to Yeshua for help, and by his good grace he will free you.

<u>MARCH 22</u>

God is always looking out for you. He uses the difficulties of life to help us grow spiritually, but he has a heart to protect you from harm. The Lord attends to your circumstances and your struggles, and when you become ensnared by sin, his desire is to see you overcome and prevail.

This is what your Lord says — the Lord, even your God, who defends his people — "Look, I have removed from your hand the cup that causes staggering; that goblet, the cup of my fury. You will never drink it again."

✡ *Isaiah 51:22*

Ironically, God sometimes uses things which are detrimental in order to draw us closer to him. When people are in trouble, then they become more likely to call out to God! But this verse promises that there will come a time when he will not ever have to use such drastic methods again.

The cup of his wrath will be withdrawn at some point. God's people will be perfectly aligned with his will. Pray to him, that *you* would be in his will today!

MARCH 23

The world we live in is fallen, sadly. Because of this, even the very best we can hope for during our time here is but a glimpse of God's glory. But if we are looking for the fingerprints of God, we may see traces yet – because even in this fallen world there is some goodness, which comes from him. Today count yourself blessed to have God on your side, cheering for you like a proud parent. He will give you the strength you need to get through each day.

"Wake up, wake up; put on your strength, Zion! Put on your beautiful garments, Jerusalem, the Holy City! For the uncircumcised and the unclean will no longer enter you."

✡ *Isaiah 52:1*

The Holy City has been battered, bruised, and conquered many times over. Jerusalem of today is just as much a product of this fallen world as any other dirty town or village. But God's work isn't through yet!

Isaiah the prophet foresaw a great day in the future, when Jerusalem will be clothed in strength, and the royalty of God will be on full display. That will be a tremendous day for all believers! If you have never been to Jerusalem, never fear. One day you will walk through its streets in the glory of Yeshua, clean and new.

MARCH 24

The gospel is a message of true hope and love. God sent his only son down to earth so that he would willingly give his own life for others – including you! You are just as loved by God as his own son is. When you relax into your prayer time today, reflect on the great generosity of God. Consider what he says about your redemption…

For this is what the Lord says: "You were sold for nothing, and you will be redeemed without silver."

✡ *Isaiah 52:3*

This verse only makes sense in God's economy. It presupposes that you were once in slavery, but that will all be in the past. You will be set free! How? By the gift of God's grace. He paid the price for your sins, giving you the freedom to approach God as a restored child of Eden, and it cost you nothing at all.

Because of his sacrifice, you will ultimately be redeemed without money. Not all the treasure in the world is worth what he is giving to you *for free*.

Today you might begin your prayers with, "Help me Lord to better appreciate the magnitude of your grace, and the sacrifice you gave for me…"

MARCH 25

God alone is our savior and our hope. No mere human being can grant eternal life. And what's more, the Lord has given us a warning, a head's up! Yeshua entered into the same sort of dirty earthy life which we deal with now, and he spoke like the prophets who came before him: All will be reconciled! No sin will escape! No child of God will be harmed!

Therefore my people will know my name; therefore they will know on that day that I am he who says: Here I am."

✡ *Isaiah 52:6*

Probably the most important phrase which all the prophets repeat is "on that day." This phrase stands as a rallying point for all prophecy. There will come a Day in which judgment and mercy will come together. It will be both wonderful and terrible. For those who trust in Yeshua, it will be the greatest Day that ever came about.

The job of a preacher is to let people know there will come a Day: *"On that Day...!"* In what ways might you warn and encourage people to prepare for the Day of the Lord? Ask him today!

MARCH 26

In some circles there is a popular tendency to understand the "bride of Christ" as being each individual believer, rather than the corporate whole. But a correct understanding has a larger collective in mind, so that the prophetic Scriptures are seen most often as dealing with the *people* of God, as a group. This *plural perspective* allows men to understand themselves not as "brides" but as subjects of the King, and friends of God. In the next few devotional entries, we will be looking at several verses from Isaiah which use the imagery of women, brides, and mothers as primary illustrations.

"Rejoice, childless one, who did not give birth; burst into song and shout, you who have not been in labor! For the children of the desolate one will be more than the children of the married woman," says the Lord.

✡ *Isaiah 54:1*

In the story of Cinderella, the final scene describes a young woman released from the oppression of her wicked step family, and welcomed into the royal family. It is a picture of someone who has nothing, but is given everything. In today's verse we learn that God can give the impossible, even bringing life from a barren womb. But the important thing to understand is, *the Lord will not allow his people to suffer forever*. Through Yeshua he has defeated death!

MARCH 27

Take some time to let God in. Ask him to settle your heart, to comfort you, and give you strength. There is only one Savoir, and he alone is able to grant you a peace that surpasses all understanding – an indescribable peace. Breathe in deeply, and exhale. Then read…

"Do not be afraid, for you will not be put to shame; don't be humiliated, for you will not be disgraced. For you will forget the shame of your youth, and you will no longer remember the disgrace of your widowhood.

✡ *Isaiah 54:4*

The key words here are *shame, reproach, disgrace,* and *humiliation.* In Yeshua you will have no more of that, ever. It will all be swept away. In fact, all those things will be forgotten, not only for you, but for all believers.

The shame and humiliation he suffered on the cross is enough to remove any sense of loss or 'widowhood' from your life. Take time to open your heart to God today. Maybe there are things which you feel you can't tell anyone, but rest easy because you can bring *anything* to the Lord, and he will receive you.

<u>MARCH 28</u>

God loves his people with an infinite strength. There is no love like his. His love is not limited by any weakness. When he loves, it is permanent, because he is the Lord.

Indeed, your husband is your Maker — his name is the Lord of Armies — and the Holy One of Israel is your Redeemer; he is called the God of the whole earth.

✡ *Isaiah 54:5*

As noted, men need not view Yeshua as their husband, or see themselves as brides. He is your Maker and King! The Lord Almighty is his name! He is your divine Creator and your true friend in heaven. The relationship you have with him is far beyond any earthly bond.

Go to him today with a trusting heart, and pray, "Dear Lord, I love you because…"

MARCH 29

Have you ever lost something, or someone, which meant the world to you? Such a loss is devastating, and we wonder how to go on. Death, divorce, fighting, and pain all take their toll on our relationships with one another. But God allows us to be in relationship with him, and there is no better One to learn from than Yeshua. He is always merciful, and always ready to reconcile.

For the Lord has called you, like a wife deserted and wounded in spirit, a wife of one's youth when she is rejected," says your God.

✡ *Isaiah 54:6*

Have your plans been ruined? Have you had your trust betrayed by a close friend? If so, you are in good company. Yeshua is calling you back to God to have your sins forgiven, and to show you how to forgive others. He will not reject you.

 In prayer today, thank God for leading you back to himself. "Loving God, you have rescued me from…"

MARCH 30

It is not always easy to connect with God when we have been running around in the world. That's why it is important to set aside time specifically for prayer and devotion. Think about what a privilege it is to approach the throne of the Living God! As you search him out, you will grow to know him better and better.

"In a surge of anger I hid my face from you for a moment, but I will have compassion on you with everlasting love," says the Lord your Redeemer.

✡ *Isaiah 54:8*

Do you find it strange to think of God as being angry, and then at once compassionate? People who don't know the Lord are often scandalized by his show of emotion in Scripture. Some might even say God is fickle! But the truth is, God has all the emotion and passion that people have, and more.

God feels anger, joy, sorrow, regret, excitement, even hatred. Our own emotions are a reflection of his, because we were created in his image. But notice, although God has *a surge of anger*, his eternal *love* is what wins out. The emotions of God never lead him to sin, they simply reflect his feelings.

If you appreciate the ardent love God has for you, allow him to permeate your thoughts today in prayer: "Dear God, please fill me with your Holy Spirit and…"

MARCH 31

Your God is immeasurably powerful. There is no other Being in the universe that compares to him. No angel or demon can hold a candle to him, because he is the One who allows all others to be gifted with even the smallest measure of power. Consider the imagery in this verse…

Though the mountains move and the hills shake, my love will not be removed from you and my covenant of peace will not be shaken," says your compassionate Lord.

✡ *Isaiah 54:10*

Mountains in the Bible are pictures of supreme strength. They stand in place long before any of us are born, and they remain long after we die. But even the largest mountains will erode long before the loving promises of God's will be shaken.

Look outside and consider the world he has made. As enduring as it appears, it will not outlast his devotion to you! In return today, give yourself to God.

<u>APRIL 1</u>

There are times in life when we forget who is in charge. We think we are! The song lyric is true: *Everybody wants to rule the world*! But when you awaken in the morning, there is only one God who causes the sun to rise, and blesses you with mercy and grace for another day. Prepare you heart as you draw near to the Lord in humility and joy.

Arise, shine, for your light has come, and the glory of the Lord shines over you.

✡ *Isaiah 60:1*

When Isaiah speaks of the glory of the Lord, he aligns it with *light*, *rising*, and *shining*. We are encouraged to rise and to shine! Why is that? Because something much greater than the sun is shining on the people of God – it's the glory of the Lord! It may be a cloudy or sunny day outside, but the glory of the Lord is illumination to your soul.

In Hebrew, "glory" is not about beams of light, but rather the *gravitas* of God – his reputation or heaviness. To say that God is glorious is to say that he is powerful, influential, and his name carries the heavy weight.

Turn to him in prayer today! Arise and shine! His glory rises upon you!

APRIL 2

The most powerful people in the world are those
who plug into the power of Yeshua. Through faith
in him, the working of the Spirit of God in the
human heart is both exhilarating and humbling. On
one hand, we know we are vessels of clay, only here
for a little while. At the same time, the strength of
the living God is moving in our lives, and no other
force on earth can counter what he is doing.
Consider this verse regarding the supposed power
of kings and nations…

*Nations will come to your light, and kings to your
shining brightness.*

✡ *Isaiah 60:3*

It is distressing to survey the times and see how
little hope and encouragement there is in the world.
Our earthly leaders – placed in power by God –
promise hope, light, security, wealth, and justice,
but themselves are so often greedy and corrupt to
the point of being evil. But the Lord is alive, and he
is unstoppable! Nothing can prevent the
overwhelming force of his kingdom from crashing
in and taking over this fallen world. All at once his
glorious light will shatter the darkness and scatter
the sin. When that happens, this verse from Isaiah
will come true in fullness.

Read it again, and store his word in your heart.
Pray vigilantly because The King is coming!

<u>APRIL 3</u>

To live by faith is to trust who God is. Trusting who God is means understanding that his word is truth, and that he will accomplish it. So when you put your faith in Yeshua, you are trusting him to save you, because that is what his name *means*, and that is who he is. He saves.

You may put your trust in other things, but they will ultimately let you down. Even the most reliable people are flawed and weak compared to him. In the biggest picture, Yeshua is the only friend you have who can rescue you from death and darkness.

While he was in Jerusalem during the Passover Festival, many believed in his name when they saw the signs he was doing.

✡ *John 2:23*

If you are tired, even exhausted, rest your head by allowing your thoughts to be filled with his goodness. You do not need to use words in order to come to him in prayer. You do not need to say anything in order to welcome him into your heart. You need only turn your thoughts to him, and allow the Holy Spirit to move within you.

God has all the power and energy you will ever need, stirring inside you, to help get you through your struggles.

APRIL 4

In the darkest hours of your life, Yeshua is there with you. When you are hurting, he is there. When you are lonely, he is there. When you are broken hearted, he is most certainly there. You can lean on him completely. You can fall upon him with your full weight, sins and all, and he will hold you up, even through the most treacherous storms. If you cling to him, in the end you will be greatly rewarded…

Then you will see and be radiant, and your heart will tremble and rejoice, because the riches of the sea will become yours and the wealth of the nations will come to you.

✡ *Isaiah 60:5*

When God is your friend you can look forward to being rescued from death and chaos, and brought into the Kingdom of the Lord. When you put your faith in Yeshua and his crosswork, you become a true friend of God, and your course is set towards the calm waters of eternal bliss. God opens the very gates of Eden to share his treasures with his children.

And when you see him at last, you will *be radiant*, with a heart swollen from joy, because you will be a part of the full restoration of Israel.

In prayer today, patiently allow the Lord to give you the words you should speak, but listen first for his leading. Maybe he has something to whisper into the quiet stillness of your heart.

APRIL 5

There is no end to the lineage of persecutors who have done evil against the people of God. His people include anyone who has put their faith in him, and joined the commonwealth of Israel. So from Haman to Hitler, from Sennacharib to Stalin, there is an unbroken history of hatred and violence directed at those who gravitate toward the God of the Jews. But one thing is clear, despite the bloody track record of history, none of it will escape the eye of Yeshua.

Consider these bold words…

The sons of your oppressors will come and bow down to you; all who reviled you will fall facedown at your feet. They will call you the City of the Lord, Zion of the Holy One of Israel.

✡ *Isaiah 60:14*

Note that even "the sons" of Israel's oppressors will bow. It is a tragic truth that evil is passed down from generation to generation. But notice also the expansive title of God's chosen city: *Zion of the Holy One of Israel!* This is no mere strip of dry land! God's influence and power will fill the whole earth, and there is no device or weapon which can touch him. He will stand up for those who have been crushed like seeds under a millstone.

Ask him to fill *you* with his Spirit now, so that you can walk the faith-walk today!

APRIL 6

There is no denying the Judaic tenor to God's plan of salvation. Take a few moments to center your thoughts on the Lord, then, when you are ready, digest this verse slowly and entirely, reading each word carefully as you would savor an excellent meal…

You will nurse on the milk of nations, and nurse at the breast of kings; you will know that I, the Lord, am your Savior and Redeemer, the Mighty One of Jacob.

✡ *Isaiah 60:16*

Isn't it reassuring to hear God's repeated descriptions of himself? Read them aloud, and allow each title to revive your spirit. God is who he says he is. "I, the Lord…"

In Yeshua he has adopted you, and will sustain you. Today you might begin your prayers as follows: "Loving Lord, I want more than anything to be a part of your plan, please help me to follow you today by…"

APRIL 7

All good things come from God. None of your needs escape him. When you come to the Lord in prayer today, calm your heart before him. Ask the Lord for a willing spirit, and an open mind, so that you might better hear and follow his leadings.

"I am the true vine, and my Father is the gardener. Every branch in me that does not produce fruit he removes, and he prunes every branch that produces fruit so that it will produce more fruit."

✡ *John 15:1-2*

The symbolism of a vineyard is recounted numerous times in the Hebrew Scriptures, most often to indicate Israel. In describing himself as the true vine, Yeshua is pointing out that everyone, even the Jewish people, must come to place their faith in him. It is not enough to be an Israeli, or an American, or some other nationality. Everyone who wants to grow must become a branch in the True Vine.

At the same time, there is a process of pruning that happens in the life of every believer. Are you willing to allow the Father to trim away certain things from your life – attitudes, desires, hopes, expectations? Pray today, "Dear Lord, please do whatever it takes to help me grow in you. Cause me to become more…"

APRIL8

As you enter into prayer today, remember the imagery from the day before: Yeshua is the vine, and God the Father is the divine gardener, pruning and tending to the growth of his vineyard. Hold onto this imagery throughout the day as you go about your business.

You are already clean because of the word I have spoken to you.

✡ *John 15:3*

In John chapter 13 while he was washing their feet, Yeshua told his disciples they were "clean, but not all of you." The text tells us he said this because he knew Judas was going to betray him. But those who *remained with Yeshua* were *already clean*, because of the things he had spoken to them.

A vinedresser has to remove dead wood, pluck off dead leaves, and snap off branches which inhibit proper growth. Once he has done this pruning, the vine is considered 'clean.' Pray today that God would help you to endure the difficult process of pruning, and that his word would take root deep inside of you. Pray as follows: "Loving Lord, thank you for making me clean. Please, cause me to remain in you..."

<u>APRIL 9</u>

We all need the cleansing blood of Yeshua over our lives. There is not a single person who is morally strong enough to walk through this world untainted by sin. Take a few minutes to let God into the private places of your heart, and allow him to focus your thoughts on good and heavenly things.

Remain in me, and I in you. Just as a branch is unable to produce fruit by itself unless it remains on the vine, neither can you unless you remain in me.

✡ *John 15:4*

Yeshua is like a friend who lends you a hand when you need it most. If you have overcome drugs, alcohol addiction, or any mean habit, you can be grateful to him for working in your life. For this reason, it is crucial to *remain* close to him. Do not jump off the vine!

Yeshua is a good influence in your life, and you *need* him. Ask him today in prayer, "Dear Lord, please show me how to stay close to you, give me wisdom and grace so that I can…"

APRIL 10

As you come to Yeshua today, close your eyes and breathe deeply. If you can hear the sound of your own heartbeat, listen for a few moments. Feel your breath filling your lungs, and call to mind The One who sustains your life.

I am the vine; you are the branches. The one who remains in me and I in him produces much fruit, because you can do nothing without me.

✡ *John 15:5*

Remaining in Yeshua is the key to your spiritual growth. You may study and learn a million things, but if you do not remain in him these things will be fruitless.

Notice also, *he* remains *in you!* Does that idea stop you in your tracks? It should. As one of his branches, he lives *inside* you. Without him thriving *in, with,* and *through* you, you are like a dry branch with no nourishing sap – no juice! But you need only rest and remain in Yeshua, and he will cause all the growing.

Today ask him to give you a restful heart. "Dear Lord, I need your shalom. Please guide me to grow in the ways you want me to grow…"

<u>APRIL 11</u>

There is never a wrong time to come to God. If you hear his coaxing call today, follow it. Have the courage to surrender your life to him. He is the only one who can give you peace and rest. If there is something holding you back, ask him to remove every obstacle. As a loving heavenly Father, he responds to your prayers before you can even give voice to them.

If anyone does not remain in me, he is thrown aside like a branch and he withers. They gather them, throw them into the fire, and they are burned.

✡ *John 15:6*

There is only one unpardonable sin – that is the rejection of Yeshua. Even a person who tragically commits suicide is only guilty of short circuiting God's plan for their life. But those who walk away from Yeshua, never accepting their own fallen state and dire need, are in peril of being thrown into the fire. A dead branch is useless. So heed the warning and encouragement of Yeshua: Remain close to him like a friend who is helping you to walk. Depend on him for your every meal, your every breath.

Today you might begin your prayers with, "Loving Lord, please help my friend who does not know you…"

APRIL 12

Prepare your heart for some time with the Lord. Know and remember that you need only abide, rest, and remain in Yeshua, the True Vine. Nothing else is required of you. He has kept you in his vineyard for another day, and you can confidence that the Divine Gardener has carefully cleaned you, and he will continue to look after you.

If you remain in me and my words remain in you, ask whatever you want and it will be done for you. My Father is glorified by this: that you produce much fruit and prove to be my disciples.

✡ *John 15:7-8*

This passage has often been pressed into the service of heretical teachings. As we all know, mankind is prone to wishing for evil and detrimental things. But God would never freely grant every evil wish spewing from the hearts of men.

The aim of Yeshua is to make you more *godly*, not wicked. As you pray properly, you will learn over time that your prayers will be answered when you are in harmony with the will of God. He wants you to pray to him, and you should feel free to tell him anything. Go ahead and so now!

APRIL 13

There is only one man in Scripture who was said to have seen God face-to-face, and that is Moses. Prepare yourself for the words of Moses set to song for the Lord. The song is recorded in Deuteronomy 32, and is said to have taken place soon before Moses' death. It represents some of the final words of the man whom God used to free the Israelites from slavery…

Let my teaching fall like rain and my word settle like dew, like gentle rain on new grass and showers on tender plants.

✡ *Deuteronomy 32:2*

It only makes sense that a person who has spent time with God would be able to impart deep wisdom in old age. If you spend time with God, he will bless you with wisdom too!

Pray as the Lord leads you today, and meditate on the imagery Moses describes. Allow the teachings of the Lord to nourish you like water to a green plant. At the same time, think ahead to your own future, and consider what the Lord has shown you, and how you might share with those younger and less experienced than yourself.

"Loving Lord, please teach me…"

APRIL 14

There is only one God, and he is flawless. No imperfection can be found in him, because he is pure and right in every way. As you enter into your prayer time today, acknowledge that you are in need. Go to him in humility. He made you in his own image, and he wants you to come to him for restoration and life. Because he made you, he knows what you need, and how best to help you.

The Rock — his work is perfect; all his ways are just.
A faithful God, without bias, he is righteous and true.

✡ *Deuteronomy 32:4*

God is not like a fickle acquaintance who does not keep his word. He is mighty and strong, like a rock. There is only one path to God – through Yeshua – but he has many facets to his personality. Yet everything he does and thinks is clean and genuine.

You can count on him when you struggle with sin, because he has cleared a path for you to approach his throne – through Yeshua! Pray along these lines today: "Dear Lord, I know I am not perfect, but you are. Please make me more like your Son, so that …"

<u>APRIL 15</u>

People often speak of "generation gaps," as if there is a disconnection between old and young people. But there should not be such a thing. In Hebrew culture the key to keeping the generations together is a godly heritage, based on walking with the Lord. Consider this profound instruction from Moses in your devotional time today…

Remember the days of old; consider the years of past generations. Ask your father, and he will tell you, your elders, and they will teach you.

✡ *Deuteronomy 32:7*

If you feel disconnected from people older or younger than yourself, pray for them today. They have struggles in life too. The truth of God is able to overcome any age gaps, and bond people together forever. We may not always understand each other, but we can come together in unity of the faith.

Pray today for those who are closest to you. "Dear Lord, please help strengthen the bonds of my relationships, because there are times when…"

APRIL 16

God will move mountains to get to you. He loves you with an unchanging heart. You may feel like God is distant from your life, but that is not the case. As his son or daughter, he will not stop pursuing you until you are safely in his kingdom. He will guide you through all the thorns and traps. Even if you suffer great pain, he will not fail to deliver you from evil. Moses describes God's soaring love...

He found him in a desolate land, in a barren, howling wilderness; he surrounded him, cared for him, and protected him as the pupil of his eye.

✡ *Deuteronomy 32:10*

This verse depicts God searching out his most prized possession – Jacob / Israel – and bringing him into his protection and care. It may also be considered messianic, applied in retrospect to Yeshua!

Has God found you and rescued you? Are you out there, feeling along in some howling desert? If so, consider that one day there will be a *Second Exodus*, when God brings you out of the wilderness. He will guard you like the apple, or pupil, of his eye. With great care and sensitivity he will make sure no harm comes to you.

In prayer today, ask the Lord to give you protection, and to prepare you for the days ahead. You too, are the apple of his eye!

APRIL 17

People often ask why God allows evil to exist. Why create a devil? And wouldn't it be better if there were no sin at all? The answer is yes, it would be better, and that is what God is aiming for in your life and mine. But God is able to use evil things for good ends. Somehow, at the end of the day, all the wrath of mankind will be to his glory. Consider the single-minded perspective Moses sang of at the end of his long life…

See now that I alone am he; there is no God but me. I bring death and I give life; I wound and I heal. No one can rescue anyone from my power.

✡ *Deuteronomy 32:39*

Moses understood that God brings death as well as life. God is love, but he also hates sin. And the Lord our God inflicts wounds, but he also heals. This is his mystery and paradox.

Consider the wounds Yeshua endured on your behalf. Somehow, in a supernatural way which we do not fully understand, God has taken full responsibility for all the evils of the world, through the crosswork of our Savoir. Evil has been used for good. If you are a follower of Yeshua, then you can praise God, and thank him for your salvation.

APRIL 18

There was a time in Israel's past when animal sacrifice was required to forgive sins. But since Yeshua has come, we have a far better way to approach God. Because Yeshua came in the image of sinful man, but not as a sinner himself, mankind was given a representative who could approach God directly and atone for our sins. Moses calls us to rejoice in God's atoning work…

Rejoice, you nations, concerning his people, for he will avenge the blood of his servants. He will take vengeance on his adversaries; he will purify his land and his people.

✡ *Deuteronomy 32:43*

Take a long hard look at your sins, and hold them up to the cross. Mourning comes before rejoicing. Do not skip over the sorrow of sin, because the joy is more real when you have felt true remorse.

When you have turned to Yeshua, do not beat yourself up. There is no condemnation coming from God for those who are in Christ Yeshua, and there should not be any coming from yourself.

APRIL 19

Begin your week with a healthy time of prayer. Renew your commitment to the Lord, and allow him to bring you into that place of peace and understanding. Ask Yeshua to prepare your heart and mind for what the Scriptures would teach you from the story of Noah. Take time to consider what this verses is saying…

The Lord regretted that he had made man on the earth, and he was deeply grieved.

✡ *Genesis 6:6*

In all your times of devotion and study, have you ever stopped to consider that God has powerful *emotions*, just like you do? It makes sense, since people were made in his image. God has 'heart' according to the Bible, and he possesses the same range of feelings we do: anger, joy, sorrow, love, hate, etc.

If that is a strange thought to you, ask him to give you his peace. He has blessed you by creating you in a way that reflects his own personality. Today, offer both your thoughts *and your heart* to him in prayer.

"Dear Lord, the thoughts of my heart are as follows…"

APRIL 20

There are certain events in our lives which shape us dramatically. For Noah, his experience on the ark would change his life permanently, even as an old man! When you pray today, try and think about the life-markers that have made you who you are. Remember how God has shaped you, and where you have come from.

God remembered Noah, as well as all the wildlife and all the livestock that were with him in the ark. God caused a wind to pass over the earth, and the water began to subside.

✡ *Genesis 8:1*

If you are ever tempted to think God has forgotten you, read this verse again and take hold of it. God *remembered* Noah. God cared about Noah enough to place him at the forefront of his thoughts. And even though there are multitudes of people, all praying countless prayers, God is able to give you his full attention.

Today you might start praying by saying, "Yeshua, help me to remember…"

APRIL 21

There are times in history when the people of God must respond to the evil around us. All have sinned, but the children of God are responsible for doing *right* whenever we can. Allow this verse, in which God speaks to Noah, to challenge you today. If the Lord calls you to respond, do not hesitate!

And I will require a penalty for your lifeblood; I will require it from any animal and from any human; if someone murders a fellow human, I will require that person's life.

✡ *Genesis 9:5*

Notice the high value God places on people. Even the animals will be held accountable! In our world today the value of a human being is considered negligible by many, but not so in God's eyes. The same loving Lord who created us in his image watches over every person, and takes note how they are treated.

Psalm 8:5 tells us people have been made, "a little lower than the angels." Those who act like base animals will be judged accordingly.

Ask Yeshua to soften your heart today, and pray for those precious people who are the most vulnerable.

<u>APRIL 22</u>

Judgment Day is in the future. How far off? God only knows. But the following passage gives us a flavor of things to come. Before you read it, make sure you have opened yourself up to the Lord. Stretch your hands apart, close your eyes, and lower your head. As you breathe, allow the Holy Spirit to fill and refresh you. When you are ready, read…

They didn't know until the flood came and swept them all away. This is the way the coming of the Son of Man will be. Then two men will be in the field; one will be taken and one left.

✡ *Matthew 24:39-40*

All too often this passage is mistakenly understood to describe the rapture. But think about the flood story – the people were suddenly swept away in *judgment*. When the authorities come unexpectedly, by night, and snatch someone away, it is not to hand out rewards.

As you consider this fallen world and the direction things are heading, pray that Yeshua's grace would inform your lifestyle. Ask him to shape you, and to guide you, so that you would learn to live a holy life, set apart in contrast to this sad world. When you put your trust in him, you will be able to help others to know the love of Yeshua, as you do.

APRIL 23

Everybody grows tired at the end of a long day. As years go by, fatigue can become a way of life! But there is One whom we must stay awake for – Yeshua! If you are feeling weary, come to him and ask for wisdom, strength, refreshment, and encouragement in the Holy Spirit. There is no good thing God will keep from you.

Therefore be alert, since you don't know what day your Lord is coming.

✡ *Matthew 24:42*

In olden days a watchman sat on top of a high tower and waited for a runner to deliver the news. Far off in the distance someone would come, tired and out of breath, to bring word of events from a remote land. As a child of God, you are a spiritual watchman, or watch-woman. Pray that he would give you the right kind of vision to see with! Also, be ready to spread the news, and stay on the alert!

Pray the following: "Dear Yeshua, help me to stand at the ready today as I …"

APRIL 24

We began the week by noticing again that God has emotions. Sometimes our own emotions can overpower us, so we either fall apart, or we kill them off. But there is a better way. Make time today for prayer and devotion. You need it, and it will be good for you.

"For this is like the days of Noah to me: when I swore that the water of Noah would never flood the earth again, so I have sworn that I will not be angry with you or rebuke you.

✡ *Isaiah 54:9*

Even though the Lord was regretful at having made people in the first place, and even though there is a coming Judgment Day, there is also a great *restoration* on its way. God's kingdom will be restored on earth, and the hostility between the Lord and mankind will be entirely erased.

Yeshua himself will rejoice with his people, and there will be no more sorrow or pain. Focus on him then, and his promise to rescue you through grace. Allow him to free you from self-condemnation, because he *loves* you. Remember that one day you will be with him face-to-face, and never again will sin cause you to fall.

<u>APRIL 25</u>

The story of Abram's calling will become the focus of our devotional time. Take a few minutes to relax, breathe deeply, and ask the Holy Spirit to fill your heart and mind. There are many things ahead which the Lord has for you to do, so put him first this week.

The Lord said to Abram: Go out from your land, your relatives, and your father's house to the land that I will show you.

✡ *Genesis 12:1*

Have you ever been called to cut ties with some aspect of your past, never to return? Spend some time considering this, but also pray about what may be preventing you from moving forward today. Are there sins which you need to run away from?

God called young Abram – a 'green' 75 year old man – to become a pioneer. Ask the Lord to guide you into your future and show you the clear path. Ask him to give you the wisdom to know which ties you should cut!

APRIL 26

To become a part of the people of God is a blessing, no matter how or where you came to know Yeshua. When you approach the Lord with a humble heart, asking forgiveness for your sin, he quickly moves in your direction, eager to take you into his fold. All of God's covenant promises are then yours to cling to, and to share with the people of God.

I will make you into a great nation, I will bless you, I will make your name great, and you will be a blessing.

✡ *Genesis 12:2*

The fact that you call Yeshua 'Lord' is what ultimately sets you apart. In him, you become part of a great nation, and a blessing to others around you. Abram set out for the Promised Land in faith, and by faith you also are his child in the truest sense. So then, prayerfully re-commit your faith in Yeshua today, and allow yourself to feel connected to Abram's legacy in doing so.

You might meditate on God's direction, and the way in which he is bringing you to places you've never been before. Use your own words, and speak from the heart.

<u>APRIL 27</u>

Modern Israel has many enemies. There is no end to the political intrigue which seeks to plague the Promised Land into destruction. But God keeps a close watch on this world, and nothing eludes his penetrating eye. Consider his great promise to Abram…

I will bless those who bless you, I will curse anyone who treats you with contempt, and all the peoples on earth will be blessed through you.

✡ *Genesis 12:3*

It seems absurd that a people who are so reviled could become the source of global blessing. But God is a loving God, and his *shalom* runs against the grain of everything else. The way in which the whole world will be blessed through Abram, is because the Savoir – Yeshua – has come into the world through him.

Pray today, and ask God to use you in ways that would bring others to the same faith you share along with Abram.

APRIL 28

Even the most devoted man or woman of faith is in need of rescue and redemption. On our very best days we still fall woefully short of the perfect morality of God. That is why he sent Yeshua – to give us a means of reconciliation to the Lord. In him, all our best intentions gone awry can be reformed. Look how Abram began his journey…

So Abram went, as the Lord had told him, and Lot went with him. Abram was seventy-five years old when he left Haran.

✡ *Genesis 12:4*

Recall what the command was at the start: "Go!" God told Abram to head out, leave the land, leave the family, and do not look back. But Lot came along, and there is no indication Abram ever tried to prevent him. By taking his nephew Lot on the trip, Abram was setting himself up for a good deal of trouble in the Promised Land, at places like Sodom and Gomorrah.

When you try to walk in faith before Yeshua, most certainly there will be those things from your past which will try to cling to you, and hold you back. In prayer, ask God to re-double your focus on him, removing *everything* which may become a hindrance!

<u>APRIL 29</u>

Many times reality does not meet our hopes or expectations. Take some time to sit before the Lord, and offer him your worries and concerns. There are so many. But you can know with certainty that he will hear your prayers, and will not leave you. Consider what happened to Abram when he arrived in the Promised Land…

There was a famine in the land, so Abram went down to Egypt to stay there for a while because the famine in the land was severe.

✡ *Genesis 12:10*

Imagine that! A *famine* in the Promised Land! Doesn't that seem wrong in every way? Yet, God uses our difficult times to shape us, as he did with 'young' Abram.

Most likely, there are aspects of your life which you find difficult, and you may even have asked the Lord to remove them. But sometimes he *uses* them instead. If God has given you a famine in the 'Promised Land,' do not be afraid. He has a plan for you that reaches well beyond your present circumstances.

Pray today for wisdom, strength, and new hope!

APRIL 30

It is sometimes easy for those of us who attend worship services regularly to come to a point where we think we are measured by what we *do*. But nothing could be further from the truth. While blessing others is important, ultimately we are measured by what Yeshua has already *finished* – in his crosswork.

For what does the Scripture say? Abraham believed God, and it was credited to him for righteousness.

✡ *Romans 4:3*

There is nothing you can do that would put God in debt to you. He owes nobody. That is why his grace is a gift; no one becomes righteous through rules and laws.

The faith-walk consists of trusting him for everything, and acting in ways that honor the Lord.

Pray today that your faith in him would be put into action!

MAY 1

The Lord has many promises for you when you put your faith in Yeshua. He will never let you fall, he will provide for your needs, he will bring you peace, and he will give you a destiny when you cross over to the grave – he will not leave you there. Today, take some time to ponder the amazing promise God has given you in the resurrection of Yeshua.

Sarah denied it. "I did not laugh," she said, because she was afraid.

But he replied, "No, you did laugh."

✡ *Genesis 18:15*

It was hard for Sarah to believe she would have a child when she was 90 years old. In fact, she did not believe it at all. She laughed at the idea!

Consider this: If you were to die today, you would wake up in the presence of God. Like Yeshua, he will give you a new body, and a pure nature, so that you would never sin again. If that sounds laughable, too good to be true, ask the Lord to take you deeper today!

"Dear Lord, I trust you for big things. I trust you for…"

MAY 2

God is faithful to the end. It may take more time than you would like, but he knows what is best for you. Sometimes waiting is the best thing for a person...

The Lord came to Sarah as he had said, and the Lord did for Sarah what he had promised.

Sarah became pregnant and bore a son to Abraham in his old age, at the appointed time God had told him.

✡ *Genesis 21:1-2*

You can bet Sarah had wanted a child for a long time. In ancient days a child meant continuity and blessing, and even today children are still a source of protection and love for the elderly. In time, Sarah's own son would grow to be her 'brother in the Lord.'

If you do not have a family, ask God to place you into one. People are not meant to be alone, so pray the he would bring believers into your life who will become family to you.

<u>MAY 3</u>

Allow yourself to rest in Yeshua. Breathe deeply, close your eyes, and give the Spirit room in your heart. Confess your needs, and prepare yourself for the word he has for you today. The more you spend intentional time with Yeshua, the more you will reflect his goodness and character.

Sarah said, "God has made me laugh, and everyone who hears will laugh with me."

✡ *Genesis 21:6*

When something great happens, do you give God credit? Do you tell others of the things he has done for you? Sarah's laughter was turned from skepticism into delight. Let the Lord be your delight today as well.

Don't get caught up worrying about the things you don't have. In his perfect time he will give you all the blessings you need. Pray along these lines: "Loving Lord, I want to laugh along with Sarah. I give my future to you…"

<u>MAY 4</u>

Growing into maturity means becoming spiritually and morally responsible for your actions. If you have struggled with sin – and everyone has – don't give up hope. Continue to walk with Yeshua, and ask him to build you up.

The child grew and was weaned, and Abraham held a great feast on the day Isaac was weaned.

✡ *Genesis 21:8*

This verse is thought by scholars to describe young Isaac's Bar Mitzvah. It is a milestone ceremony to celebrate a child's coming of age. In our modern society we need to bring back the Bar and Bat Mitzvah, because it is important to recognize what God is doing in the life of a young person. It is important to celebrate spiritual growth, and to let young people know they have reached a place of greater moral responsibility.

If you personally have never received such recognition, do not fear. At some point the Lord himself will say to you, in front of all creation, "Well done, my good and faithful servant."

<u>MAY 5</u>

If you knew what the future held, would you be so eager to get there today? Sometimes we are so anxious to move on from where we are, we forget to be thankful. Before you head out to do the dailies, take some time to thank God for some basic things: Food, a warm bed, hope, and whatever comes to mind after you read this haunting verse…

After these things God tested Abraham and said to him, "Abraham!"

"Here I am," he answered.

✡ *Genesis 22:1*

This is the section of Scripture where God asks Abraham to sacrifice his son, Isaac. If Abraham knew what the day would hold in store, how would he have approached that day?

"Here I am!"

Abraham had spent a lot of time with God, praying, walking, and sharing life. Hopefully, over time, you will become the same way – alert to the call of God in your life, just like Abraham. And when God leads you into threatening times, you will be able to hear his voice calling out to you!

<u>MAY 6</u>

In the end, after we have undergone trials and tribulations, heartbreak and pain, God will remain true to his word. You can count on him. Now there is a certain place in Jerusalem which is hotly contested: The temple mount. On that spot is where Abraham is said to have offered Isaac as a sacrifice, where God prevented him from doing so, and instead provided a substitute in his place…

And Abraham named that place The Lord Will Provide, so today it is said: "It will be provided on the Lord's mountain."

✡ *Genesis 22:14*

Take that promise to heart in prayer today. Repeat and memorize it: "On the mountain of the Lord it will be provided." God promised Abraham a son. He promised that Sarah would become pregnant. And he has also promised *you* a future, and the golden hope of his kingdom, in Yeshua.
Remember: *On the mountain of the Lord it will be provided!*

<u>MAY 7</u>

In the grand scheme of things, all that you have comes from the Lord. Spend a while in solitude, meditating on Yeshua, and allowing the Holy Spirit to fill your mind and heart. This week you will have an opportunity to reflect on the ways in which God has blessed you.

Abraham was now old, getting on in years, and the Lord had blessed him in everything.

✡ *Genesis 24:1*

Whether you are old or young, a journey with God will only enrich your life. You may earn or lose money along the way, you will have your ups and downs. But in the end you will be spiritually wealthy for having spent years in the presence of the Lord.

Pray today, "Almighty God, thank you for the ways in which you have guided me and helped me to grow. Thank you for…"

MAY 8

In this life there are situations you must avoid if you are to walk the true path before Yeshua. It is easy to be distracted and lead astray if you are not paying attention. See how Abraham sent out his servant on an important mission...

"...and I will have you swear by the Lord, God of heaven and God of earth, that you will not take a wife for my son from the daughters of the Canaanites among whom I live."

✡ *Genesis 24:3*

When you have found the best path, take it! Do not play around with things you know are only going to harm you. Sometimes it seems we only learn things the hard way, but if you are in the midst of big decisions, do not rush into making a bad one. Take the time to pray, and seek God's wisdom so that you do not make rash vows, and ensnare yourself.

Today you might begin praying along these lines, "Dear God, please keep me from causing myself more trouble than necessary. Help me to search out your direction today..."

MAY 9

Sometimes the thing we want is waiting right around the corner. Sometimes all we need to do is be patient. And quite often, God knows much better than we do when the right timing is…

"Before I had finished praying silently, there was Rebekah coming with her jug on her shoulder, and she went down to the spring and drew water. So I said to her, 'Please let me have a drink.'"

✡ *Genesis 24:45*

When the Lord brings about a divine appointment, be willing to make a change! Rebekah went to water camels, only to find the servant of her future-husband ready to take her home.

Trust God to show up in your daily routine today. You never know what might make *this* day important!

<u>MAY 10</u>

Being prepared for the Lord is a lifetime practice.
One day you will meet him face-to-face. Ask him
to fill you with his peace and strength today, and to
protect your faith…

*Rebekah looked up, and when she saw Isaac, she
got down from her camel and asked the servant,
"Who is that man in the field coming to meet us?"*

✡ *Genesis 24:64-65*

Rebekah saw Isaac – her future husband – way off
in the distance, and did not want to spoil the
moment. She hid her face until the big day.

In what ways is God calling you to protect your
own innocence? There are a lot of wicked things in
the world, and many paths run into harm. But if
you pray for protection, Yeshua will preserve you
until the end. And if you feel you have been
damaged, ask him to restore you by his grace and
love.

<u>MAY 11</u>

When life hands you major changes, be sure to lean on the Lord. There is only one God, and he is looking after you all the time. Consider what happened to Isaac during a major turning point in his life…

And Isaac brought her into the tent of his mother Sarah and took Rebekah to be his wife. Isaac loved her, and he was comforted after his mother's death.

✡ *Genesis 24:67*

Sometimes God takes away things we love, only to bring about changes that we need. In the end he is always faithful. The pain we endure today will be a forgotten memory in the kingdom of heaven.

Is God making changes in your life? Ask him to help you cope with new situations. Nothing is permanent, and God has a plan to bless you. Pray for his peace today.

MAY 12

Have things been rough lately? Fortunately the mercies of God are renewed every morning. Make a determined effort to do the right thing today. Consider old King David, near the end of his life…

King David responded by saying, "Call in Bathsheba for me." So she came into the king's presence and stood before him.

The king swore an oath and said, "As the Lord lives, who has redeemed my life from every difficulty, just as I swore to you by the Lord God of Israel: Your son Solomon is to become king after me, and he is the one who is to sit on my throne in my place, that is exactly what I will do this very day."

✡ *1 Kings 1:28-30*

When things life gets tough, keep your promises, pay your dues, and be a servant.

Start to pray today like so: "Dear God, help me to finish my race strong. I trust you with…"

MAY 13

Prepare yourself for the Lord, and allow his peace to fill you. Move quietly through your daily ritual of prayer and thanksgiving to Yeshua. You are blessed to be one of his children, and there is nothing that can snatch you away from him. This week you will learn from the negative lessons of Jacob's brother Esau. Consider this prophetic verse…

And the Lord said to her: Two nations are in your womb; two peoples will come from you and be separated. One people will be stronger than the other, and the older will serve the younger.

✡ *Genesis 25:23*

This passage centers on God's sovereign choice to reverse the order of the birthright. He does this several times, with Isaac and Ishmael, with Joseph and his brothers, and also here in the account of Jacob and Esau: The younger son will receive the blessing.

Sometimes God does the exact opposite of what we might expect! Are there ways in which he has done so in your own life? Reflect on how he has helped you through sudden fortune or misfortune.

Pray, "Dear Lord, help me to trust your choices for my life…"

<u>MAY 14</u>

Spend a few minutes in silence before Yeshua. Breathe deeply, and let the Holy Spirit focus your thoughts on him. Consider this: When you were born, God brought you into this world with specific intention. He knew who you were, and who you would grow to become. This is a blessing! But not everyone appreciates this…

Jacob replied, "First sell me your birthright."

"Look," said Esau, "I'm about to die, so what good is a birthright to me? "

✡ *Genesis 25:31-32*

Thank God today that your own birthright involves being his son or daughter through the crosswork of Yeshua! His sacrifice sets you on a permanent path to the kingdom of God.

Allow the Lord to shape your view of who you are. He knows you better than you know yourself, and it is best to let God chart your course because he will protect you and preserve you until the day he *perfects* you.

Pray, "Loving Lord, keep me in your will and on the right path today. Show me the ways in which I need to grow and trust you more…"

MAY 15

Have you ever made a mistake that seemed to have endless repercussions? Impulsivity can cause us to do things we never should do. Consider another sad misstep of Jacob's older brother Esau…

When Esau was forty years old, he took as his wives Judith daughter of Beeri the Hethite, and Basemath daughter of Elon the Hethite. They made life bitter for Isaac and Rebekah.

✡ *Genesis 26:34-35*

Thank God for his grace today, that you can come to him and ask for help coping with your own mistakes! Give him all your concerns, and worries. If you have done damage to others, make amends to the best of your ability, but trust the Lord to resolve the things you have no control over, as well as the missteps you have made.

Ask God to give you resolve, so that you can walk through this life with the knowledge that he will not give up on you. Pray like so: "Dear Lord, I regret my sins, so I trust you to move me forward…"

<u>MAY 16</u>

Sometimes people add to their own problems by making one poor choice after another. It becomes a downward spiral which is hard to escape from. But God can change your life by breaking the vicious cycle, and helping you mend the rips you have caused. Take time to consider the way in which Esau makes things even worse for himself through intentional disobedience…

Esau realized that his father Isaac disapproved of the Canaanite women, so Esau went to Ishmael and married, in addition to his other wives, Mahalath daughter of Ishmael, Abraham's son. She was the sister of Nebaioth.

✡ *Genesis 28:8-9*

Esau clearly stands as a negative example, someone to avoid emulating. He made very bad decisions, and then compounded them one on top of another. Do not allow yourself to be tempted to seek revenge by harming yourself. God loves you! And there is a Savior who can wash you clean every morning.

Are there some issues you seem to struggle with that you cannot break free from? Yeshua will never give up on you. Keep praying, keep coming back to him. Do not look to others for perfection, look to him alone. Continue praying along these lines: "Dear Lord, please keep me from…"

MAY 17

Everyone has some degree of mess in their lives. It doesn't matter who you are, eventually you will have your own personal bag of mess. But in Yeshua you can have release. In him there is the hope for a future which is free and clear. After calming your heart, allow this passage to renew your larger perspective…

"My name will be great among the nations, from the rising of the sun to its setting. Incense and pure offerings will be presented in my name in every place because my name will be great among the nations," says the Lord.

✡ *Malachi 1:11*

Take note that God has expectations for the *future*. The promises of the prophets are just as resounding and uplifting as they ever were. If you find yourself bogged down in the mud of life, do not despair – you have an advocate in heaven. Take the time today in prayer to allow God's promises of the *future* to become your governing reality.

You might begin by praying, "Dear Yeshua, I want to invite your kingdom to break into my personal life. I offer you my…"

MAY 18

If you feel you have foolishly traded your own birthright for something broken, do not give up hope. God can turn things around, and bring life from the dead. He is more than capable of setting you on the right path, even if you have been on the wrong one for many years. Consider this great promise...

That is, it is not the children by physical descent who are God's children, but the children of the promise are considered to be the offspring.

✡ *Romans 9:8*

Through Yeshua, you are a child of the promise. When you fall – and everyone does – be quick to return to him. His promise to you is still alive, and he will answer your prayers. If you have ever felt like Esau, take heart. God does not hate you. He wants to lift you up into a new life altogether. You may have harmed other people, and even harmed yourself. But the King of Kings is a friend of yours, and you do not need to live in the past.

Approach the Lord in humility and faith, trusting his wisdom, and he will call you blessed – a part of the family of God through Yeshua.

MAY 19

If there is one thing you can trust, it is the faithfulness of God. Friends may abandon you, people may let you down, but the Lord is always with you, and he will be true until the end. Today, make it a point to focus fully on him. Determine in your heart that you will pray as regularly as possible, and bring to him all your cares and concerns.

"Look, I am with you and will watch over you wherever you go. I will bring you back to this land, for I will not leave you until I have done what I have promised you."

✡ *Genesis 28:15*

This is God's promise to Jacob, after he had dreamt of a ladder into heaven. Many years later, walking with a limp, God would indeed bring Jacob back to the very same spot where he first had the dream.

In the same way, God will bring you to himself gradually over time, and when you finally move from out of this life and into the next, he will be there to meet you in person. In prayer, ask the Lord to aid you in your journey.

"Dear Lord, sometimes I feel as though I've come full circle. Please walk with me today, and bring me to…"

MAY 20

Have you ever suddenly come to the realization that God is always with you, even when have been unaware? This can be convicting! But through the Holy Spirit he is always attending to your life, guiding and protecting you. Take time to consider Jacob's reaction to a prophetic dream from the Lord...

When Jacob awoke from his sleep, he said, "Surely the Lord is in this place, and I did not know it."

✡ *Genesis 28:16*

If you have ever had a vivid dream, and wondered if it was from God, be extremely careful. God has spoken to us primarily and uniquely through his word, so our dreams can be very misleading. Do not assume a dream of yours is from God, but rather, ask him for wisdom when you have questions.

In this vein, you might pray along these lines today, "Dear Heavenly Father, please protect me from superstition and conspiracy. Even so, I want to worship you in spirit and in truth, as Jacob did. Today I ask you to help me see you more clearly in the following areas..."

<u>MAY 21</u>

This life can be strange and confusing, but it is a gift from God. There are many things we do not understand, and it is normal to have more questions than answers. But there is One who cares for you deeply, and he is sure to put you on the right path: Yeshua! Before you pray, consider for a moment how God describes his love for his people, Israel, and what tenderness he has for those who are his own...

I led them with human cords, with ropes of love. To them I was like one who eases the yoke from their jaws; I bent down to give them food.

✡ *Hosea 11:4*

The picture of a little child is meant to conjure in your mind an idea of how dependent you are on God, and how much he loves us – with ties of love. As his children, we are in constant need of support and reassurance, and he is there to give it. Have you ever been so tired and confused that you didn't know which way to turn? Turn to him today! He can lift your chin like a hungry child, and give rest to your weary heart. Find your security in him.

Pray like so: Loving Heavenly Father, help me today. I need you, and I know I cannot make it on my own. Please help me as I struggle with..."

<u>MAY 22</u>

God hates injustice, because he cares for the down trodden. When you care for those in need, you are doing the work of Yeshua. When you protect the vulnerable, you are also doing the work of Yeshua. When you share the truth of the cross, you are bringing the love of the Holy Spirit. Think about how protective God is over his people when you read this amazing verse from Hosea…

A sword will whirl through his cities; it will destroy and devour the bars of his gates, because of their schemes.

✡ *Hosea 11:6*

Over thousands of years, God's people – the Jews – have been persecuted and killed. There has never been a time when the world did not hate the people of God, and history is a sad list of atrocities, handed down over time, becoming worse with each passing generation. But one day, the sword will flash in the opposite direction; those who spread lies in the name of God will be stopped dead in their tracks. All the scheming and hatred directed at God's people – both Jews and Gentiles – will be no more.

Throw yourself at the foot of his throne in prayer today. No matter what happens, he will be there, protecting you.

<u>MAY 23</u>

We have a merciful and strong Savior. Take some quiet time for you and him alone. Clear some space, and settle your heart. If there is anything troubling you, ask the Lord to set your mind at ease. You are with him, and he is there with you, in a peaceful place. Now, imagine yourself back in the days of John the Baptist, walking along the seashore. The wind is blowing, the sun is hot, and the sound of crashing waves fills your ears. Then suddenly this happens…

The next day, John was standing with two of his disciples. When he saw Jesus passing by, he said, "Look, the Lamb of God! "

✡ *John 1:35-36*

Your Lord, Yeshua, is ultimately all-powerful. There is no one in the universe stronger than he is. Yet somehow he appears figuratively as a lamb. He could have come as a warlord and conqueror, but instead he came gently into the world. One day he will return to take back what is his, but even in the book of Revelation he is seen at times as a slain lamb. He does not conquer the same way earthly kings try to.

Today you could begin your prayers with, "Dear God, please make me gentle like you. Make me humble and willing to be weak, so that you can be strong in my life. Help me to recognize you in…"

MAY 24

Yeshua gives hope to everyone who comes to him. When we read about Jacob we found that he had a sudden realization that God was with him, even as he slept! But when Yeshua walked the earth the very presence of God became tangible and physical to the rest of us. The Lord even went as far as to say the following…

Then he said, "Truly I tell you, you will see heaven opened and the angels of God ascending and descending on the Son of Man."

✡ *John 1:51*

If there is any stairway to heaven at all, it is Yeshua. He is the only way. Trust his word, trust his promise. His crosswork where he shed his blood is able to save you and set your destiny toward the Kingdom of Heaven.

One day, when your time here is finished, the angels will greet you. All this is because Yeshua paved the way for you to climb the stairway as well. Pray today, "Thank you Lord, for everything you have done for me. Thank you that I have peace with you, along with…"

MAY 25

Today you have a bold new opportunity to choose to walk *in* and *with* Yeshua. Take a stand today by praying from the deepest core of your soul. The Lord *is* with you, he *does* love you, and he will give you everything you need to overcome trials and pass the tests you encounter. Fortunately, the Bible is filled with examples for you to learn from. Prayerfully consider Jacob / Israel, and how he dealt with his own personal weakness, yet lived out his faith anyway.

"You are also to say, 'Look, your servant Jacob is right behind us.'" For he thought, "I want to appease Esau with the gift that is going ahead of me. After that, I can face him, and perhaps he will forgive me."

So the gift was sent on ahead of him while he remained in the camp that night.

✡ *Genesis 32:20-21*

Jacob was a deceptive child from his youth. He had stolen his brother's birthright, and ran away to escape his wrath. Many years later he was faced with a new encounter with Esau, and in the dark of night Jacob was terrified at the thought. Have you ever had to deal with something from your own past which came back to haunt you? God is right there with you in your fear and concern. Pray today that he would teach you through *grace*, rather than through fire. Yeshua died so that you can live free!

MAY 26

God knows you better than you know yourself. It's true. Sometimes that is comforting, but sometimes that may bother you. You may wonder why God allows certain things to happen in your life, and it may not seem fair. To be truthful, often times life is *not* fair, and so we look to God for help. If you have ever wanted to scream out – and ask God, "Why me?!?" – consider Jacob once again, and the way he encountered God...

Jacob was left alone, and a man wrestled with him until daybreak.

✡ *Genesis 32:24*

In his fear of Esau, Jacob sent everyone and everything he owned ahead of him, across the Jordon River. When he was all alone, "a man" came and wrestled with him.

Have you ever wrestled with God in your own way, all by yourself? If not, on occasion you should! Because God can take it! In fact, he would rather have you wrestle with him, than throw in the towel and give up. Life is hard, the Lord knows it, and lots of our biggest questions do not get answered. So today, if you have complaints and troubles, *wrestle with God* over some of those difficult issues which are giving you problems. When you are done praying and wrestling, he will still be there with you.

MAY 27

In your weakness, Yeshua is strong. Hold fast to him with all your might, and eventually you will understand that *he* is The One giving you the strength to hold on.

Consider what happened to Jacob in his refusal to let go of God…

When the man saw that he could not defeat him, he struck Jacob's hip socket as they wrestled and dislocated his hip.

✡ *Genesis 32:25*

Some injuries are God-given. Consider the harder lessons he has allowed you to learn, and pray: Is there someone who might be blessed, and even benefit, through your injury? Is there someone with whom you might share the reasons for your own limp…?

God is always there to hear your cries of pain. Ask him to use these experiences to help build up other believers.

MAY 28

Wrestling with God on occasion inevitably helps us grow. When we wrestle with God he sees our passion and desire to know him better. Rather than being lukewarm and apathetic towards Yeshua, it is better to be hot or cold. When you wrestle with him, even out of your frustration, he sees within you a great longing to break through, and he honors that.

Then he said to Jacob, "Let me go, for it is daybreak." But Jacob said, "I will not let you go unless you bless me."

✡ *Genesis 32:26*

Jacob refused to let go of God, even after his hip had been wrenched out of its socket! But his wrestling hold was no longer intended to force "the man" into submission. Now Jacob held on for dear life. He was no longer focused on his own fears, or on Esau. He knew he needed the blessing of the Lord, his Savior, so he would not let go. That is the kind of clarity that comes when you wrestle with God.

In prayer today, *wrestle with your God.* Do not give up until you have received his blessing. Hold on for dear life – he is your life raft! When you are done, ready to face the world, remember who walks with you, even as you limp along.

MAY 29

Honesty before God is essential to understanding where we stand spiritually. If you cannot come clean before God, who can you be honest with? The only human being who ever walked a perfect walk is Yeshua, and we can be thankful he has blazed a trail for us to follow.

A big part of the faithwalk is understanding where we stand, and admitting we need help from the Lord. When Jacob was finally brought into submission before God, he was faced with the deepest question regarding his identity…

"What is your name?" the man asked.

"Jacob," he replied.

✡ *Genesis 32:27*

Jacob's name meant *deceiver*, and that is who he was. Jacob had deceived Esau, he had even deceived his own father, but he could not fool God. Neither can we.

He knows our names, and he knows our fallen natures. When the Lord asked Jacob what his name was, it may have been that Jacob felt ashamed. After all the years of doing things his own way, he was suddenly handicapped, and holding on for dear life. Your inner life is important because it pours out of you, so take the time today to come clean with Yeshua. He died for your sins, so you have a safe harbor to seek refuge. He will not turn you away, but before he blesses you, he will ask you to face who you are inside.

MAY 30

The only way to have true joy in this life is to get right with God. He welcomes repentant sinners with open arms. All you have to do is turn to him, and trust in the crosswork of Yeshua. Once you have admitted your need of his mercy and grace, he will remove your guilt and replace it with freedom. He will change you from the inside. Someday he may even change your name!

"Your name will no longer be Jacob," he said. "It will be Israel because you have struggled with God and with men and have prevailed."

✡ *Genesis 32:28*

On a national level the people of Israel have endured overwhelming abuse and persecution, but on a personal level you can be grateful today that, through Yeshua, you are an overcomer. Because of him, you *will* conquer in the Spirit. He will win the battle for you, and you will celebrate with him.

Pray today, "Dear Lord, help me fight the good fight by…"

MAY 31

Take a load off your shoulders, and put it down at the cross of Yeshua. There are times when you need to set aside everything else, and seek his company. Set a table for two, and be ready to meet with your God! He has always been faithful to meet his children when they seek his face.

By faith he stayed as a foreigner in the land of promise, living in tents as did Isaac and Jacob, coheirs of the same promise.

✡ *Hebrews 11:9*

You too are an heir of the promises God gives to his people. And similarly, like Abraham, Isaac, and Jacob, you live in a 'tent' of sorts – your temporary dwelling place on this earth.

The founding patriarchs of our faith are long gone, but they live forever in the presence of God. One day, when your own tent is ready to be discarded, you will also be in the presence of God, and he will present you with a new resurrection body. When that day comes, neither you, nor the patriarchs, will ever be strangers in a foreign land again.

JUNE 1

At times you may feel out of place in the world. Sometimes even the familiar people and places can unsettle a person. Then the reality dawns on us – this world really isn't your permanent home at all. The city you live in, the place where you sleep, is all temporary. Even the sky above may be torn down one day, when the King returns.

For he was looking forward to the city that has foundations, whose architect and builder is God.

✡ *Hebrews 11:10*

When a believer trusts the future to the Lord, that means he, or she, cannot see what the future holds. We would like to pretend we know, but we really do not. Yet even the greatest city you can imagine cannot compare to what God is able to build for you. That's the promise of God, and that is the unseen hope he is preparing for you. To have *faith* means you trust him, and you look forward to entering the city he is constructing, *sight unseen.*

JUNE 2

It does not matter who you are, God cares about you, and loves you. What's more, love does not hold bias toward age, gender, color, or capacity toward sin and / or holiness. All people are feeble, and in need of salvation through Yeshua. He does not look down on anyone who comes to him with an open, believing heart. Also, he is still a God of miracles.

By faith even Sarah herself, when she was unable to have children, received power to conceive offspring, even though she was past the age, since she considered that the one who had promised was faithful.

✡ *Hebrews 11:11*

You may not experience the kind of seemingly impossible miracle that Sarah did, but then again, you never know. Perhaps you may! You have an entire lifetime to walk with God, and there is every reason to trust that you will experience small miracles on occasion, done on your behalf, to help you along the way.

All this is part of the larger promise, that God will ultimately deliver you, if you trust him with your life.

JUNE 3

Abraham is a fine example of biblical faith. In
Genesis 15:6 we learn that Abraham believed God,
and in turn, God considered Abraham to be
righteous – set right with God. For the child of
God, the journey of faith is an upward trajectory.
Even the worst life has to offer will ultimately be
turned into glory and celebration, one day, when the
King brings us all home. So it makes sense that
occasionally, when it matters most, and when we
really need it, God will show us what he can do in
our lives.

*Therefore, from one man — in fact, from one as
good as dead — came offspring as numerous as the
stars of the sky and as innumerable as the grains of
sand along the seashore.*

✡ *Hebrews 11:12*

The descendants of Abraham, his many children,
include yourself. You probably feel very small
when you stop and consider this reality. But
imagine how Abraham will feel, someday, meeting
you face to face, and learning that you are a part of
his family of faith. Even more, imagine the both of
you – Abraham and yourself – sitting down with
Yeshua for a family meal.

Our God is truly a God of miracles, both big and
small!

JUNE 4

Again, it's time to draw near to Yeshua. Ask the Father to fill you with the Holy Spirit, and let him enter your heart. Tell the Lord about your week. Tell him about the struggles you had, the concerns, and hopes. The faithwalk is one of trust, fear, nerves, and joy, all rolled into one – the agony and the ecstasy! Even though the darkness closes in, and our days are few, we are not hopeless people. We are, what they used to call, *sojourners*. We are passing through, on our way to someplace better. And we are not alone…

These all died in faith, although they had not received the things that were promised. But they saw them from a distance, greeted them, and confessed that they were foreigners and temporary residents on the earth.

✡ *Hebrews 11:13*

The reason those people of faith, who died before you were ever born, passed through this world but did not attain the wonderful rewards promised by God, is so that you and I could catch up. We came along later, but God still wants us there in the Kingdom with him, all together. We are all on our way to *another realm*. The place you are headed is a royal and divine Kingdom, filled with wonderment and the radiance of God. If you could catch a small glimpse of it today, you would not want to return to ordinary life. Then again, until our time comes, we have work to do for the King!

JUNE 5

Amidst all the upheaval and noise in the world, it is very comforting to know that God will always hear your prayers. He knows you, he loves you, and he is superintending all the events of this world, including your life. Give yourself some time to breathe, pray, and settle your heart. The Lord is not in a hurry, and his pace is different from ours. You can trust him to be there at any hour of the day or night.

"Comfort, comfort my people," says your God. "Speak tenderly to Jerusalem, and announce to her that her time of hard service is over, her iniquity has been pardoned, and she has received from the Lord's hand double for all her sins."

✡ *Isaiah 40:1-2*

This passage represents the mid-point to the book of Isaiah. It represents such a dramatic shift, away from condemnation, that scholars have traditionally thought there may be two Isaiahs. Regardless of what the case may be – the great Isaiah scroll from the Dead Sea is a single literary work – the Lord wants his people to hear the message clearly: At a certain point in time all the trials and tribulations will be over with, and his comfort will come upon us.

Ask him today for that inner comfort and shalom that only comes from Yeshua.

<u>JUNE 6</u>

As the seasons change, and your life unfolds, the Lord will use many important events to shape you. Sometimes those things you wish did not happen end up being the best things that ever happened, because they draw you closer to God in new ways, and bring new dimensions of richness to your life, which otherwise you would have missed. At the same time, some of the things you may wish for are best left out, because the Lord has a greater plan for you. Young Joseph had exactly these sorts of up and down experiences…

Then Pharaoh sent for Joseph, and they quickly brought him from the dungeon. He shaved, changed his clothes, and went to Pharaoh. Pharaoh said to Joseph, "I have had a dream, and no one can interpret it. But I have heard it said about you that you can hear a dream and interpret it."

"I am not able to," Joseph answered Pharaoh. "It is God who will give Pharaoh a favorable answer."

✡ *Genesis 41:14-16*

If you are faithful to God, and trust his direction for your life, there will be times when you can look back on your hardship and be grateful that he brought you through. Granted, you will not ever want to go backward, but you can always go forward in a new way. Today, ask God to give you a long perspective on the problems you face. Trust that some good can be wrought from out of your hardships, and ask him to teach you to pray!

JUNE 7

There are no guarantees in life. Sometimes we have to wait, in faith, and trust God to work things in our favor. Truth be told, there are blessings which can come your way when you least expect it. Joseph did not expect to be plucked from the dungeon, after many years of humdrum isolation, and then to be called on to give godly wisdom to the Pharaoh.

So Pharaoh said to Joseph, "Since God has made all this known to you, there is no one as discerning and wise as you are. You will be over my house, and all my people will obey your commands.

✡ *Genesis 41:39-40*

Consider that Joseph had been sold into slavery by his own brothers. The people who should have been the most protective of him – his own family members – betrayed him. Now, many years later, he was only one rank lower than a king. God took him from the prison to the palace, in one quick move. Most of life can be uneventful, until that day when God calls you to stand and deliver. Today, pray that God would prepare you for those crucial times when you can be used for kingdom purposes!

<u>JUNE 8</u>

After surviving a crisis, it is easy to carry our wounds around for the rest of our lives. God does not want us to forget the past, but his healing answer is always out there, in the future. Look how Joseph celebrated what God had done for him even in Egypt…

Joseph named the firstborn Manasseh and said,
"God has made me forget all my hardship and my whole family."
And the second son he named Ephraim and said,
"God has made me fruitful in the land of my affliction."

✡ *Genesis 41:51-52*

In what ways can you commemorate and celebrate what Yeshua has done for you? Ask God to show you traces of goodness in this fallen world, so that you can be thankful like Joseph was.

Mark out the monuments in your life, which help you remember God's faithfulness. Pray to Yeshua, "Dear God, I have always needed you…"

JUNE 9

Joseph may have thought his painful past was far behind him. Then one day his brothers showed up in his neck of the woods, looking for food. Times were desperate, and it was a long trip from Judea down to Egypt, but in order to survive people will go to great lengths. So his treacherous brothers left the Promised Land, and went down to Egypt, which was the bread-basket of the Middle East. However, one of them remained behind…

So ten of Joseph's brothers went down to buy grain from Egypt. But Jacob did not send Joseph's brother Benjamin with his brothers, for he thought, "Something might happen to him."

✡ *Genesis 42:3-4*

It makes sense to be protective of your child. Every loving parent would agree. But Jacob did not know that he would be required to send Benjamin on the next trip! Yet this was how God worked, in order to bring them all back together in a tearful reunion.

Is there something dear to your heart that God has called you to trust him with? Do not hold anything back. If God calls you to do something frightening, take consolation in the fact that he is always with you. Ask today, "Dear Lord, is there something I refuse to let go of? Show me! And please show me how. Here and now I give you the following…"

<u>JUNE 10</u>

Take a few moments to settle your heart before Yeshua. He has given everything for you, so that you can have everything in return. His goodness and mercy are gifts to you, and your joy is rooted in his unfailing love. Do you recall a time when you were outside of the will of God, before you came to faith in Yeshua? No doubt God has brought you through some big changes. You have let go of some things, and embraced others. Imagine seeing your old self in a mirror…

Although Joseph recognized his brothers, they did not recognize him.

✡ *Genesis 42:8*

Because Yeshua died for your sins, you can be certain of your destination. You are becoming a new person, headed for the Kingdom of Heaven, because of what he did. Nothing can ever erase what he has accomplished on your behalf.

Today, if you could look into the face of a loved one who has passed on, and see his or her new body in full glory, you would not recognize that person at first. The transformation God is going to complete in your life is going to be dazzling. And that is something to look forward to, and thank God for!

JUNE 11

When everyone else is doing the wrong thing, it is easy to get sucked into the same bad behavior. But when you wise up, it is important that you do the right thing, even in the face of peer pressure. Consider how Judah finally came to take some responsibility…

Then Judah said to his father Israel, "Send the boy with me. We will be on our way so that we may live and not die — neither we, nor you, nor our dependents. I will be responsible for him. You can hold me personally accountable! If I do not bring him back to you and set him before you, I will be guilty before you forever.

✡ *Genesis 43:8-9*

This same Judah helped sell Joseph into slavery years before, but now he is the one who sets his father's heart at ease, and brings Benjamin down to Egypt.

Have you reached a point where you are sick of participating in the evils of the world, and you want to become a true man or woman of God? Pray today about the ways in which God had called you to step up, and determine to do those things before it is too late!

JUNE 12

Spiritual maturity grows gradually, over time, and sometimes with much pain. Begin your devotional time today by making yourself still and quiet before Yeshua. You are in his presence. Once you have allowed the Holy Spirit to fill you, breathe deeply and consider what Judah said to his younger brother Joseph…

Now please let your servant remain here as my lord's slave, in place of the boy. Let him go back with his brothers. For how can I go back to my father without the boy? I could not bear to see the grief that would overwhelm my father."

✡ *Genesis 44:33-34*

At a certain point in life you will come to understand that other people are dearly important to God. Judah, after selling his brother into slavery, took on responsibility later in life, after years of growth and time to reflect.

You too may have regrets from your years of living, but God is able to restore you by his grace, if you allow him – if you can personally own your sin. Pray today that Yeshua would cleanse you of all sin, and give you the strength to stand up for righteousness when your time comes.

JUNE 13

One of the many reasons prayer is crucial to spiritual growth, is that it allows you to remember who is in control – God! When the hard times come, he is there. Sometimes he will allow the unexpected to occur, in order to shake us out of our complacency. And sometimes life deals us some very hard blows. Consider Joseph's strong reaction, when he heard Judah plea on behalf of his father, Israel.

Joseph could no longer keep his composure in front of all his attendants, so he called out, "Send everyone away from me!" No one was with him when he revealed his identity to his brothers.

✡ *Genesis 45:1*

Joseph was an adopted authority figure in Egypt, almost royalty. As such, his demeanor was supposed to be calm, strong, and dispassionate. But when he heard about his Dad, whom he had not seen in years, he came undone.

God does not expect people to be robots, without emotion, even though part of the fruit of the Spirit involves self-control. Do not let a crisis be the only thing that causes you to devote time to Yeshua. Spend time with the Lord today, so that you will know where to turn tomorrow!

JUNE 14

God made our emotions, and they are good, even if they seem to get in the way at times! We were meant to feel, as God himself does. In times of great stress we can become so overwhelmed that we forget ourselves. Nevertheless, your Heavenly Father is there to comfort you, and there is nothing he cannot handle. Consider Joseph once again…

But he wept so loudly that the Egyptians heard it, and also Pharaoh's household heard it.

✡ *Genesis 45:2*

Have you ever had an experience shake your foundations? It may seem like everything is out of control, but the Lord is there to comfort you. He will hear your every prayer!

If you are troubled at all today, cry out to Yeshua!

JUNE 15

Over time *the world* may shape you into something very different than what you might have expected a long time ago. If you could meet face-to-face with yourself as a child, would the younger you want to be the person you have become today? Hopefully you have not lost your way. God allowed the world to transform Joseph from a Jewish shepherd boy into an Egyptian ruler. But at a certain point the whole facade fell apart…

Joseph said to his brothers, "I am Joseph! Is my father still living?"

✡ *Genesis 45:3*

When a great moment of truth arrives, and you stand before Yeshua with nothing to hide, do you know who your true Father is? You may have had a great earthly father, or a lousy one, or maybe an absent one. But your Heavenly Father is the one who cares for your inner identity, and he is still very much alive.

Devote your heart to him today. Continue the following prayer: "Loving Heavenly Father, teach me who I am in you…"

JUNE 16

The spiritual life involves seeing God work even in the most vexing circumstances. You may not have ever been sold into literal slavery, but perhaps you have felt betrayed. Maybe you have been stepped on. If you have been around long enough, certainly you will feel diminished and hurt on occasion by someone close, who has turned on you. But hindsight gives us a chance to see God's vindication…

And now don't be grieved or angry with yourselves for selling me here, because God sent me ahead of you to preserve life.

✡ *Genesis 45:5*

Notice how Joseph tells his brothers not to become distressed or angry for selling him into slavery so many years prior. Only a person who has overcome hardship and been healed by God can honestly say such a thing. Joseph was able to see the good work God was doing – saving lives – through the long road which transformed him into an Egyptian ruler. If you cannot recognize something similar in light of personal events which have hurt you, take time today to ask Yeshua to work deep inside your heart. Some things take a great deal of time, and God does not expect you to be perfect in this life. Even still, he will never abandon you. So pray with an expectant heart!

__JUNE 17__

When God gives you an opportunity to reclaim a part of you that was lost, do not hesitate. Jump at the chance. He made you, he loves you, and through Yeshua he is in the process of making you whole. See how quickly Joseph put things in motion...

Therefore it was not you who sent me here, but God. He has made me a father to Pharaoh, lord of his entire household, and ruler over all the land of Egypt.

"Return quickly to my father and say to him, 'This is what your son Joseph says: "God has made me lord of all Egypt. Come down to me without delay.'"

✡ *Genesis 45:8-9*

By his grace, there will come a time in your life when you can honestly say, without a trace of irony, that the most painful events in your life were the very things that brought you the closest to God. You may lose everything, but he will never leave you. You may be jailed, injured, dismissed, or hated. If so, remember Yeshua. Hurry to him quickly, and do not wait. He is there with outstretched arms, happy to have you back home, where you belong.

JUNE 18

Entering into a new season of life brings both excitement and challenge. Sometimes we look at the path ahead and do not see God. That is okay. The faithwalk involves trusting him when the road ahead is dark. Spiritual growth comes from waiting on the Lord even when you do not see him in your life. Take time to quiet your thoughts, breathe in, and exhale. When you feel his shalom come over you, consider the fear which took hold of Joseph's brothers. Imagine how you feel when you have sinned.

When Joseph's brothers saw that their father was dead, they said to one another, "If Joseph is holding a grudge against us, he will certainly repay us for all the suffering we caused him."

✡ *Genesis 50:15*

After Jacob / Israel had passed away, Joseph's brothers were sure they would be thrown in jail or executed. After all, they had sold him into slavery, and he was fortunate to survive. But Joseph was a man of mercy, so his brothers had nothing to fear. Similarly, it is amazing how fearful we can become when we think God is out to get us. But your loving Heavenly Father is on your side, and you are forgiven through the crosswork of Yeshua. Today, start your prayer along these lines: "Dear God, sometimes I feel so afraid. I ask you to give me confidence today, because I know you are faithful and loving…"

JUNE 19

It is a new day, and you have a fresh chance to walk with Yeshua. He is good! And you have a promising future ahead of you because he has blazed the trail to life eternal. Clear away everything for a while, and allow God to focus your mind. Think about him. Think about the way he has taken away your sins. His forgiveness is a great relief, and a source of your truest joy.

But Joseph said to them, "Don't be afraid. Am I in the place of God?"

✡ *Genesis 50:19*

Joseph forgave his brothers, even after they had sent him off to a foreign land, in the captivity of strangers. He would have been justified to hang them. Instead, he forgave. What astonishing forgiveness! It takes a great heroic faith to forgive someone who does you grave harm. That is the kind of forgiveness followers of Yeshua are called to, even though we are wise to protect ourselves (and others) from harm.

Today, ask God to help you forgive like Joseph did, and like Yeshua did.

<u>JUNE 20</u>

Sometimes we can *see* God working so clearly in our lives. It does happen, once in a while, and we can clearly recognize it, (not always!), but sometimes it is very clear, and when it is *we know it in our hearts*. The challenging part for us is perspective. We see evil, and have a hard time trusting that good will come from our circumstances…

You planned evil against me; God planned it for good to bring about the present result — the survival of many people.

✡ *Genesis 50:20*

On this day, pray for a heavenly perspective. You do not want to sugar coat all the bad things in life, but there is a larger story going on, and you never know what may happen. Anytime something good comes out of evil, you know it is God at work.

Today, ask the Lord to show you how to pray, and how to see things from his grand view. You will be amazed at the way he changes your heart and mind.

<u>JUNE 21</u>

Before you charge out the door, take time to approach God in prayer. Ask for a quiet, peaceful, and humble heart. He will always answer your prayers when you ask for wisdom. He has a big plan for you, and you will do much better after a time of devotion and prayer. One of the greatest things about our Lord, is that he welcomes us back over and over again, no matter what we may have done.

Therefore don't be afraid. I will take care of you and your children." And he comforted them and spoke kindly to them.

✡ *Genesis 50:21*

Joseph treated his brothers in a way that seemed contrary to justice. He showed them mercy. Since you are a follower of Yeshua, the Messiah, you do not need to fear the wrath or justice of God. Like Joseph to his brothers, the Lord has shown you mercy.

Today, in your place of prayer, breathe deeply, and thank God for his great and beautiful act of mercy in your life. When you are ready, tell him everything.

<u>JUNE 22</u>

Whether you are old or young, God will not forsake you. In your times of trouble he is there, always, no matter where you are in life. At the end of Joseph's life he passed on a very important message to his family, one which you should reflect on as well…

Joseph said to his brothers, "I am about to die, but God will certainly come to your aid and bring you up from this land to the land he swore to give to Abraham, Isaac, and Jacob."

✡ *Genesis 50:24*

The covenant promise of God to his people, Israel, is eternal. He will not allow his children to go extinct, and he promised to unite all of his sons and daughters throughout time, with Yeshua, at the great wedding feast of the Lamb. The children of Israel will *not* be left in Egypt, and he will not forget *you* either.

Praise God he has a special place for you as well! Someday your time will also come, and you must be willing to depart from this world as Joseph did, encouraging others in the faithfulness of God. In your prayer time today, allow the Lord to shape your thoughts about your life. Ask him for the mind of Yeshua.

JUNE 23

Today, as you prepare for what lies ahead, let the Holy Spirit enter into your thoughts, and ease your mind from the stresses of life. Give it all to him. Give him your fears, your worries, your anxieties – ask Yeshua to give you his shalom in return. The troubles you face are only temporary, even though they seem never ending. Moreover, this world is not your home, as Joseph reminded the children of Israel…

So Joseph made the sons of Israel take an oath: "When God comes to your aid, you are to carry my bones up from here."

✡ *Genesis 50:25*

By making the Israelites carry his bones up out of Egypt, Joseph was giving them a tangible reminder that they were headed out for the Promised Land. The same is true for you. You will not live as a slave to sin in this dirty world forever. God will surely come to your aid, and you will be packing up, and heading home one day. There is a place waiting for you at the end of your journey. But for now, pray once again that Yeshua would accompany you in your adventure today.

JUNE 24

The God of the Bible is supremely powerful. Nothing sustains him, apart from his own will. He was not created, and there was never a time when he did not exist. Today, prepare to encounter the Lord of all, and to ponder his immeasurable greatness. Set aside a few moments to invite the Holy Spirit into your heart, to calm you, and to fix your thoughts on him. Imagine Moses, and old man, walking through the desert, and having his first encounter with the living Lord.

Then the angel of the Lord appeared to him in a flame of fire within a bush. As Moses looked, he saw that the bush was on fire but was not consumed.

✡ *Exodus 3:2*

This miraculous event must have mystified Moses. What sort of bush, what sort of fire, can continue to blaze without going up in smoke? The imagery God wants us to appreciate is one of *self-sustenance*. God sustains himself, burning brightly, yet without being burned, or needing any other fuel for the fire. Meditate deeply on that today.

Begin to pray like so: "Dear Lord, nobody else sustains *you*, but I thank you today for sustaining *me* through Yeshua…" Continue the prayer on your own.

JUNE 25

Let God guide you today in your prayer time. Be silent before him for a time, and allow the Holy Spirit to silence the noise in your head. You are about to approach the Lord, and this time is sacred. Through Yeshua you are a friend and a child of God, and thanks to his crosswork, you are invited to draw near to the Maker of the universe.

"Do not come closer," he said. "Remove the sandals from your feet, for the place where you are standing is holy ground."

✡ *Exodus 3:5*

As a follower of Yeshua, the Holy Spirit burns alive within you, everywhere you go. Even when you fall into sin, the Lord is there, taking up residence in your heart and pulling you through. For that reason, the place you are sitting right now is holy ground as well. In fact, the entire Earth belongs to the Lord. Maybe taking off your shoes right now would be appropriate!

Offer up a prayer of thankfulness to God today. Thank him for providing a way for you to confidently draw near to the Holy One of Israel – through Yeshua.

JUNE 26

As you pray today, consider what it means to be *holy*. It is an archaic word, but "holy" means *unmixed*, or *pure*. In other words, entirely pristine and uncontaminated by sin. The God of the Bible is indeed *holy*, and he sees everything, and everyone, as either holy or unholy. And because we are sinners, God instills fear into our hearts…

Then he continued, "I am the God of your father, the God of Abraham, the God of Isaac, and the God of Jacob." Moses hid his face because he was afraid to look at God.

✡ *Exodus 3:6*

Moses rightfully feared for his life, and did not look at God. But notice the authoritative but familiar way in which the Lord describes himself: I am the God *of your father…*" In other words, "Moses – your Dad knew me, and I know you!" Moreover, through Yeshua we are able to see God face-to-face, and one day we will.

Start praying like this today, "Loving Heavenly Father, I thank you for making me holy in Yeshua, as you are holy…"

JUNE 27

There is no need to worry, says Yeshua, about what you will eat, or wear. The Lord will provide for your needs. He is not some distant giant in the sky, looking down on you with contempt. Rather, he is your loving Heavenly Father, and he attends to your welfare better than any earthly father ever could.

Then the Lord said, "I have observed the misery of my people in Egypt, and have heard them crying out because of their oppressors. I know about their sufferings.

✡ *Exodus 3:7*

This verse depicts a caring Lord, who inclines his ear toward his children. If you have ever heard a baby crying, you know what it sounds like to hear someone in need. The Lord sees you that same way, careful to make sure you are safe and sound. Even when he allows us to experience pain, is it not with callousness. When we hurt, God hurts with us and for us. But he also knows what the *finished person* will be like, and what it will take to get you there.

Is there something in your life which is causing you to suffer? Do not give up. Pray to God, and trust that he is there with you today, even when it really hurts.

JUNE 28

Sometimes people use the expression, "I'm only human." And it is true. But consider what that means. *Only* human? Every person is made in the image of the God of creation. There is no such thing as only, or merely, human. Your life matters! With God on your side, you are a child of the King of Kings, even in your weakness and insecurities…

But Moses asked God, "Who am I that I should go to Pharaoh and that I should bring the Israelites out of Egypt?"

He answered, "I will certainly be with you, and this will be the sign to you that I am the one who sent you: when you bring the people out of Egypt, you will all worship God at this mountain.

✡ *Exodus 3:11-12*

When God is with you, there is no need to fear mankind. The world is a mess because of mankind, but God is still in charge of the universe. Today he is with you too. Remember that! Memorize it! Tuck that truth inside your heart and protect it. When you are nervous or worried about a situation, remember the steady words of God: *I will be with you!*

<u>JUNE 29</u>

The God of the Jews holds the entire universe in his hand like a fragile teacup. Everything that occurs, good and bad, wondrous and ordinary, is worked out in his grand design, and there is no event which escapes his awareness. Among all the idols and objects worshipped by misguided human beings, isn't it great to know the Lord of Lords has made himself known to you?

God replied to Moses, "I AM WHO I AM. This is what you are to say to the Israelites: I AM has sent me to you."

✡ *Exodus 3:14*

As we saw with the burning bush, God is self-sustaining – He *is*. There was never a time when he did not exist, nor will there ever be. As your day unfolds, take time to give praise and thanks to God for what he has done for you. The self-sustaining God sustains you, protects you, knows you, walks with you, and loves you. What could be better than that?

JUNE 30

In your years of growing and living, you will no doubt come upon times when you fumble over your words. Someone will confront you, or intimidate you, and you will not know what to say in response. The best thing you can do is take a lesson from Moses, a man who was not the best speaker. God instructed him to do the following…

You must say whatever I command you; then Aaron your brother must declare it to Pharaoh so that he will let the Israelites go from his land.

✡ *Exodus 7:2*

God told Moses to speak the words he heard from the Lord. By listening to God, Moses would know what to say. For those of us who live today, the surest way to really hear from God is to read his Word, and learn it. By studying the Bible you not only become literate in the lessons of Heaven, you also come to know the *personality* of God himself, a great honor.

Today and this week, spend some extra time in your Bible. The Lord has a message for you written in those pages, and he loves you so much that he wants to give you that gift.

JULY 1

In times of trouble you may feel scared of powerful people. You may feel small. But no matter how terrible they may be, God is sovereign over all rulers and kings. There is no world leader, no powerful tyrant, and no hateful dictator who can overcome the Lord. Also, his people are under his divine protection. Never forget that! You can trust in the knowledge that God is dealing with evil, and nothing escapes his notice…

But I will harden Pharaoh's heart and multiply my signs and wonders in the land of Egypt. Pharaoh will not listen to you, but I will put my hand into Egypt and bring the military divisions of my people the Israelites out of the land of Egypt by great acts of judgment.

✡ *Exodus 7:3-4*

Some people, like Pharaoh, refuse to soften before God. They are determined to stand against the very One who created them! God does not ask us to have perfect understanding, or a complete knowledge of him, or of this world.   Instead he asks us to have just a little bit of faith. That's all.

You may not see great miracles in your lifetime, but you surely will see small ones. When you do, give thanks to God for watching over you. Pray today that your own heart would be wide open to his love and grace.

JULY 2

In hard times we often long for a break. Then, when good times come, it is easy to forget about the bad. Through all the ups and downs, the hills and valleys of life, one thing you can look forward to is The Day when God will reveal himself fully to mankind. This is the promise of the Scriptures…

The Egyptians will know that I am the Lord when I stretch out my hand against Egypt and bring out the Israelites from among them.

✡ *Exodus 7:5*

As Jews, we can look back to our past and see God at work. But as followers of Yeshua we can look forward to a second deliverance – a New Exodus out of sin and the sufferings of this world. One fine day the Lord will again stretch out his hand against the enemies of his people, to lift us all out of the grave. When he does, there will be freedom and joy like never before.

Today, as you go about your routine, pray for a bigger vision of this world, and consider your place in Salvation History. You are a part of something greater than you know.

JULY 3

We all struggle to do the right thing. It is easy to cut corners, to cheat, and to go along with a crowd headed in the wrong direction. Without question there will be times in your life when doing the right thing – the godly thing – will get you into trouble with other people. But pleasing God is infinitely more important than pleasing people. If doing the right thing means stirring up controversy, then take another lesson from Moses and his brother Aaron, as they set out to rescue the children of Israel…

So Moses and Aaron did this; they did just as the Lord commanded them. Moses was eighty years old and Aaron eighty-three when they spoke to Pharaoh.

✡ *Exodus 7:6-7*

Picture these two old guys, side by side, setting out to tell a powerful world ruler what to do! Sometimes it takes eighty years until we finally learn to stand strong for God, but *don't wait that long!* Practice obeying the ways of Yeshua now. Ask God to make you strong but loving, principled but merciful, steady but forgiving. It is a life-long lesson!

Complete this prayer, "Loving Heavenly Father, in what ways can I stand for you? In what ways can I be self-sacrificing like you?"

JULY 4

Today, begin your devotional time with some silence. Give your thoughts to Yeshua, and let him in. The Holy Spirit will give insight and wisdom to you, if you allow the truth of Yeshua to direct your life. If you listen to God, you will find yourself with spiritual treasure that is worth more than all the riches in the world.

But when Pharaoh saw there was relief, he hardened his heart and would not listen to them, as the Lord had said.

✡ *Exodus 8:15*

In an earlier verse (7:3), God told Moses that he would harden Pharaoh's heart. Here, in 8:15, we see Pharaoh harden *his own* heart, once things got a little easier. But because he chose to harden his heart, he was not able to really hear the helpful warnings of Moses and Aaron. Such a fooling response! He put his own life at risk, along with his people, and in the end his son was taken from him.

God does not play around when it comes to protecting his people. Take comfort in the fact that you are one of His! Ask him to guide your prayers today.

JULY 5

History is replete with examples of persecution of God's people, both Jews and Christians. There have been martyrdoms, executions, gassings, beheadings, crucifixions, and all forms of terror. But again, nothing escapes the notice of God, not even the smallest thing, and certainly not the most brazen atrocities. The Hebrew prophets were intensely concerned with justice, and they spoke of the future with clarity of vision and hope.

They will live there securely, build houses, and plant vineyards. They will live securely when I execute judgments against all their neighbors who treat them with contempt. Then they will know that I am the Lord their God.'"

✡ *Ezekiel 28:26*

Each and every person is called to experience painful days. But those days will pass away like a blurry dream. One day you will walk through the gates of eternity, and wake up in the Kingdom of Heaven. Yeshua will welcome you there. You will live in safety, with a new body, and your life will prosper forever in the shade of the Tree of Life. In that time and place, everyone will know God personally.

He is available to you in prayer today, but then he will be available for you to speak with, to touch, and to see. Pray as he leads.

JULY 6

As you begin another day, trust that God will walk with you wherever you go. If you have hopes and expectations, give them to Yeshua. No matter what comes your way, win or lose, he will always guide you into the light of his mercy and freedom. Even if you have been restless, you can take comfort from the fact that he loves you. Consider what kind of dire measures he takes in the effort to move sinning people to repent…

Then the Lord said to Moses, "Stretch out your hand toward heaven, and there will be darkness over the land of Egypt, a darkness that can be felt."

✡ *Exodus 10:21*

Imagine that kind of darkness – so dark that it must have felt like a heavy blanket. When you think about the difficult times, when things have been so dark you could practically feel it, isn't it a great relief to know that the light of Yeshua is there for you? Any time of day or night you can call out to him, ask him to help you, and he will always hear your prayers. Even in your darkest hour, he will show you mercy.

Re-commit your heart today, and allow him to bless you with the freedom that comes from life in him.

JULY 7

When you go about doing your daily routine, you will undoubtedly come across people who do not know the Lord. They may be kind people, friendly people, and even very generous and loving. But God makes a distinction between those who are his, and those who reject him, even if their rejection is deep inside. Look at the difference between the Lord's treatment of Egypt and Israel…

Then there will be a great cry of anguish through all the land of Egypt such as never was before or ever will be again. But against all the Israelites, whether people or animals, not even a dog will snarl, so that you may know that the Lord makes a distinction between Egypt and Israel.

✡ *Exodus 11:6-7*

When you put your faith in Yeshua, you become a part of the larger people of God. And he shelters his people with peace. Yes, there will be hardships and tears, but he will bring you into the Promised Land when all is said and done. Your final destiny will not be marked by death. Instead, he will give you joy, freedom, favor, and his everlasting love.

In prayer, ponder the gift you have been given, and remember the seriousness of the calling on your life.

JULY 8

Has there ever been a person in your life who influenced you in a positive spiritual way? For a moment, go back in time to where you were then, and remember why you became a follower of Yeshua in the first place. Thank the Lord for putting spiritual mentors in your path, and when you are ready, learn this verse and make it your very own…

On that day explain to your son, 'This is because of what the Lord did for me when I came out of Egypt.'

✡ *Exodus 13:8*

Who do you know today that might benefit from you sharing your own experience? Is there someone who comes to mind that needs the same guidance you needed when you were in his or her shoes? Pray about that. The Lord has done great things for you! You could be just the person to help a younger one out. How did you come to leave your own 'Egypt?'

JULY 9

It is possible, after many years of toil and trouble, to feel as if there is no goodness in the world. Yet, in the deepest darkest depths there is still hope, because the Lord is with you even when you sink into the mud. The book of Jeremiah is the same way. It takes a lot of searching to find an ounce of hope, but when you find it, hold on tightly!

"But even in those days" — this is the Lord's declaration — "I will not finish you off.

✡ *Jeremiah 5:18*

The Bible teaches us that a Day is coming – a great and terrible Day. We don't know how far off it is, and we don't know exactly how it will unfold, but we have been told by Yeshua to keep our lamps filled with oil, because it will be dark and destructive.

Yet the mercy of God is a healing ointment for your heart. Despite all the disaster mankind wreaks, God will still show mercy, he will not finish you off. Even if we deserve the same judgment that fell on Egypt, God will show mercy to his people. Take a breath, and let out a sigh of relief!

JULY 10

If you are one who thinks deeply about God and his ways, you will undoubtedly come to a point where you wonder – how can a good God allow so many evil things to occur? In fact, the Bible answers that question by turning it around. It is not God who does evil, it is man. And yet we still have a right to ask: Why would God, being good, allow evil at all? Wouldn't it have been better to make things perfect? Paul addresses this problem…

What should we say then? Is there injustice with God? Absolutely not!

✡ *Romans 9:14*

It does not seem fair that bad things happen to good people. But the rain falls on every person, and so does the opportunity to receive Yeshua by grace. Ultimately, even though terrible things happen in this world which never should occur, he has taken full responsibility for it through the cross. The crosswork of Yeshua is where God does justice. Is God unjust? Absolutely not; not at all. He sent his Son for your sake.

Pray for strength in the hard times, and remember the big picture: The Lord loves you, and he will not forget about you. Continue with this prayer, "Loving Lord, thank you for showing me mercy…"

JULY 11

God is in control even though life is chaotic. In fact, the Lord seems to allow chaos in order to demonstrate his sovereign power, even in situations which appear entirely uncontrollable. And yet, he likes *order*. When the world was first made everything was formless and void, dark and empty. But God imposed light and order on the chaos. In the same way, he allows people to live chaotic lives, undisciplined and far from him, in order to demonstrate his mercy toward those who have learned to lean on him…

So then, he has mercy on whom he wants to have mercy and he hardens whom he wants to harden.

✡ *Romans 9:18*

If a person hardens his or her own heart toward the Lord for long enough, he will allow them to pick their own regrettable path. But when you put your life in the hands of Yeshua, he will never let you go.

Today, if there is something heavy on your heart, give it to him. Let the Lord remove your guilt. He has shown you mercy through Yeshua, so take hold of it. Because of the forgiveness that comes by his sacrifice and resurrection, you are on the path to freedom. Pray like so, "Loving Heavenly Father, I need you now and always…"

JULY 12

Godly leadership starts with wisdom, and ends with the willingness to follow through when things get tough. It takes courage and heart. In the coming days we will read from the victory song of Deborah, and consider how this female judge took a gusty leadership role in the salvation story of God's people. Deborah fought the good fight, and when it was all over she made the following observation…

When the leaders lead in Israel,
when the people volunteer,
blessed be the Lord.

✡ *Judges 5:2*

Good things happen when God's people are willing to stand up. Deborah had to rally the troops to fight off an evil ruler – Sisera – and in the end they defeated him. But it took encouragement and bravery. Deborah's example gave the people someone to follow. She looked past the armies of Sisera, and saw the possibilities of victory with the help of God.

Today, pray over areas in your life, and in your community, where bravery is needed. Ask Yeshua to give you wisdom, and the heart to lead the charge wherever he may direct you.

__JULY 13__

In the face of an evil fallen world, it may seem like victory is impossible. Sometimes we wonder how good can ever prevail. But take a lesson from Deborah the judge: Boldness in the face of impossible challenges comes from the Lord. And when a willing servant-leader step forward to fight for righteousness, God should get all the glory…

Listen, kings! Pay attention, princes!
I will sing to the Lord;
I will sing praise to the Lord God of Israel.

✡ *Judges 5:3*

Notice how Deborah commands kings: "Listen!" Deborah understood that victory was only possible through the Lord. And though she was a woman – a second class citizen back then – she praised God because he is worthy of a victory song.

If you feel second class, remember who your God is! Remember whose side you are on, and remember who you belong to. Through Yeshua, God will give you victory, and he will help you to bring the good fight to a world in need.

JULY 14

One aspect of biblical leadership which runs throughout the Bible, is the fact that every man or woman of God hearkens back to what the Lord has done in the past. By remembering what he did before, you can trust that he will be here in the present and the future too. In Deborah's victory song she recalls her spiritual heritage on Mount Sinai…

The mountains melted before the Lord,
even Sinai, before the Lord, the God of Israel.

✡ *Judges 5:5*

God was there for his people in Egypt, he was there for his people when they entered the Promised Land, he was there when Deborah fought off Sisera, and he is ever-present today in your life, and in the lives of his people worldwide. There is still a God over Israel who shakes the mountains!

Let your mind rest on this truth: The Lord is powerful enough to win the battle. Evil will be defeated, never to return. When you put your trust in Yeshua, he will see you through to the end, and you will look back with joy in victory.

JULY 15

Anyone can be used by God. No person is too small, no life is inconsequential. When you take a stand against evil, the Lord is always on your side. Sometimes you may think of yourself as weak and powerless, but in Yeshua your weakness is strength, and your faith is powerful.
Look again at the way Deborah sizes herself up…

Villages were deserted,
they were deserted in Israel,
until I, Deborah, arose,
a mother in Israel.

✡ *Judges 5:7*

A mother is a protective person. She is loving but fierce. As a defender of Israel, Deborah inspired the troops to charge down Mount Tabor and win. Spiritual strength comes from the Lord, and only he can give you the steadiness to rise and confront evil.

Today in your devotional time, pray that God would make you a willing warrior after the model of Yeshua. Ask Yeshua to raise you up, and make you a life protector as well.

<u>JULY 16</u>

When Israel defeated the armies of Sisera, the final victory blow was dealt by a woman named Jael, or *Yael*. Many women are named after her in Israel today! Yael was a typical woman living her life, minding her own business, when Sisera staggered into her tent. First she lured him to a resting spot, and lulled him to sleep with milk. Then she quietly crept over, and …BANG! She pounded a tent peg right into the side of his skull. It is a gruesome tale, but evil loses, and God uses a normal woman to defeat a wicked king. Deborah sings about Yael's victory, and praises the Lord for it in song…

Lord, may all your enemies perish as Sisera did.
But may those who love him
be like the rising of the sun in its strength.

✡ *Judges 5:31*

There is nothing wrong with wanting to see evil destroyed. In fact, we are called to love the good, and hate evil just as much. Yael saw an opportunity to strike a blow for righteousness, and she turned the tides of war. Would you be willing to drive a spiritual tent peg into the evils that beset you? You may never have a tyrant wander into your home, but perhaps you struggle with drugs, alcohol, unfortunate relationships, or addictions which you cannot overcome. Ask the Lord to point out clearly the sins and habits in your life which you need to take a hammer and tent peg to.

JULY 17

It may seem ironic to some people, but peace only comes when war is waged against evil, and evil is defeated. The challenging part is discerning between good and evil to begin with! Sometimes as people of God we are called to look directly at evil and call it what it is, and we may be tempted by fear to shrink back. Never fear! The Lord is with you.

And the land had peace for forty years.

✡ *Judges 5:31*

Note how peace comes *after* a gutsy victory, but it only lasts forty years. In every generation people must rise up again, like Deborah and Yael, and confront the enemies of God. A shepherd protects his sheep, and the people of God are called to be protective of others as well. Evil will continue to rear its ugly head again and again, until the day Yeshua returns for the final battle. He will judge like no other before him, and his peace will last forever and ever.

Pray today that the Lord would instill within you his peace.

<u>JULY 18</u>

In Matthew 22, an expert in Torah asks Yeshua, "Which is the greatest commandment?" Yeshua responds with a two-fold answer: *Love the Lord, and love your neighbor.*

God commands us to *love*, and love is an action verb. Yeshua then told the man, "All the law and the prophets hang on these two commandments." So how do we understand God's law, viewing it through the lens of love? Consider the following…

Do not murder.

✡ *Exodus 20:13*

Avoiding murder (and hatred) is the bare minimum a person can do. But avoiding evil is not the same as *doing good*. Yeshua called us to *do* the golden rule: Love the Lord, and love our neighbor. By understanding the Torah through the lens of love, we may avoid murder, but we can actively love by *protecting life*. To actively prevent murder and protect life is an act of love toward God and man.

In prayer today, ask the Lord to show you other ways in which you can *do* the golden rule, by loving, and by protecting life.

JULY 19

When you come to Yeshua in prayer, he makes time for you. He always makes time for you, even when you rush around and forget he is there. Yeshua is delighted to be in fellowship with you. After you have settled your thoughts and calmed your heart before him, consider another of the Ten Commandments, and how it may be lived out by understanding Torah through the lens of love…

Do not commit adultery.

✡ *Exodus 20:14*

Adultery destroys marriages. It is indeed a sin, and very harmful. Avoiding adultery is the very least you can do. But how would you put the higher law – the command to love – into practice, in light of this command? Seen through the lens of love, the prohibition against adultery can be turned into a positive action: *Protect marriage.*

In what ways can you show love to God and mankind by protecting marriage? Pray over this today, and allow Yeshua to speak deeply into your heart.

JULY 20

The truth is sacred to God. In contrast, the devil is called 'the father of lies.' So when you think about the way God views truth, remember that it is holy to him. Lies are harmful, as anyone who has fallen victim to vicious lies can tell you. Here is the direct command from God regarding lies…

Do not give false testimony against your neighbor.

✡ *Exodus 20:16*

God expects people to avoid lying. But he expects his children to go one step further by *doing* the golden rule: Love!

By speaking truth in love, we are able to do more than stay out of trouble and avoid lying. Instead of harming our neighbor, we bless him or her.

Is there someone whom you need to stand up for? *Do* the golden rule: Speak the truth about that person in love, and set the record straight. Even if it means going against the grain of popular opinion, the Lord will reward you for defending truth and keeping it sacred.

JULY 21

How easy it is to be tugged in several directions. Life is busy, and sometimes we can become overwhelmed with so many advertisements and attempts to grab our attention. But the Lord, Yeshua, is there for you, to help calm your troubled mind, and soothe your tired heart. Breathe deeply and sit before him for a moment. When everything else is swept away, isn't it great to know the Lord is always there for you? In the end, nothing in this world can give you the peace that comes from knowing Yeshua.

Blessed are the pure in heart, for they will see God.

✡ *Matthew 5:8-3*

Being *pure in heart* means there is no division inside. Nothing in this world – no riches, or prizes, or temptations – can be allowed to take the place of the Lord inside a pure heart. When King David prayed, "Create in me a clean heart, O God," he was asking that all other things be removed, and that God alone would be at the center of his life. That is how God wants your heart as well. He wants you to love him wholeheartedly.

In your devotional time today, ask the Holy Spirit to fill your heart. Over time he will work inside you, until one day when he calls you home, when the time is just right. On that day, with a purified heart, you will be blessed, and you too will *see God* just as Yeshua promised.

<u>JULY 22</u>

Most people like peace. Peace allows for safety in life, the opportunity to work quietly, and to do well overall. But without peace all those things are gone. In the absence of peace there is strife, rage, animosity, and discord. When there is no peace, people act out in dangerous ways, and innocent people are threatened. That is why Yeshua says the following…

Blessed are the peacemakers, for they will be called sons of God.

✡ *Matthew 5:9-3*

Notice it does not say, "Blessed are the peace-lovers," or "Blessed are the peace-keepers." To be a peace*maker* is more risky. A peacemaker is someone who actually steps into non-peaceful situations, and takes necessary steps to *bring* peace where it may not even be wanted. That can be a risk! But Yeshua says peacemakers are blessed, and they will be called children of God.

As difficult as peacemaking might be, ask God to give you the attitude of a peacemaker. You may even be called to broker peace today!

<u>JULY 23</u>

The ultimate example of someone who loved, and who stood right before the God, is the Lord himself – Yeshua. He took the punishment for our sins upon himself. He allowed his body to be nailed to a cross, and willingly let his life drain out. People taunted him, they spat on him, and they beat him. Yet he tolerated it. He permitted evil mankind to kill him, the only sinless individual who ever walked the face of the earth. He knew it would happen, yet he taught his disciples the following…

Blessed are those who are persecuted because of righteousness, for the kingdom of heaven is theirs.

✡ *Matthew 5:10*

Should the day come when you should fall under the boot, verses like this will come to your mind. If you spend time with him in your secret place of prayer, he will come to your aid with words like those above. You may be in pain today, persecuted in ways you could not have imagined, but if you stand for Yeshua the kingdom of heaven belongs to *you.*

<u>JULY 24</u>

The faithwalk is filled with trouble and challenges, but the joy that is our heavenly destination is worth every tear. Sometimes the ordinary world is enough to wear us down to the point where we forget how magnificent our God is. In the days ahead we will look at several verses which put us in touch with the supernatural wonder of God's power. Take some time and be still, ask the Holy Spirit to fill you, and then ponder this passage…

When Moses went up the mountain, the cloud covered it.

✡ *Exodus 24:15*

Receiving a visible, tangible appearance of God's presence was a great gift to the Israelites who left Egypt. No doubt there are many today who would love to see such a miracle. But Yeshua appeared and walked among his people, and that is an even greater gift. So for those of us who live in the aftermath of the cross, we can draw great comfort and hope from Yeshua himself, who said, "Blessed are those who have *not* seen, and yet have believed!"

Ask God to give you spiritual sight, and open the eyes of your heart.

JULY 25

There is something fearful about the presence of God. As sinners, we are not prepared to stand before holiness. All of our problems, issues, and faults lay bare before him, and nothing prevents God from knowing our every action and thought. And yet, *he loves us*. Take some time and imagine what it would have been like to stand before the mountain of God personally, back in the days of the Exodus…

The appearance of the Lord's glory to the Israelites was like a consuming fire on the mountaintop.

✡ *Exodus 24:17*

It is easy to wish we could see God, but anybody who has come into close contact with the Lord is deeply convicted and fearful. That is because his power and holiness are a threat to our sinful ways. Peter said to Yeshua, "Depart from me, for I am a sinful man."

A consuming fire will burn up sin, and leave only what is holy. Pray today that God would do the work within you, by the power of the Holy Spirit, to make you able to stand!

JULY 26

Wherever you go, the Lord is there with you, working in your heart, and guiding your steps. You need never be concerned about the final outcome of your personal story – it will be a *happy ending* with Yeshua. God has always been faithful to help his children get where they need to go, even during the difficult time of wandering in the desert…

"I am going to send an angel before you to protect you on the way and bring you to the place I have prepared."

✡ *Exodus 23:20*

This passage is considered by many to be messianic, reflecting the coming of Yeshua. In the same way, he has prepared a place for you; he will guard you along the way, and bring you home. The most important thing for you to do? *Listen to what he says!*

In prayer today, make it a point to listen to the Lord speaking to your heart. Be very still and silent for a little while. But remember – not everything that comes into your thoughts is from the Lord, so check everything against the Scriptures! When you are ready, pray as he leads you.

JULY 27

In times like these it is important to realign yourself with the heart of God. Be still and hopeful. Remember your Savoir! He is The One who gave his life for you, and blazed the path for your salvation. One day you will see him face-to-face, in all his glory. The disciples of Yeshua had the great honor of walking with him during his earthly ministry, and seeing him up close. On one occasion they were even privileged to see his glory breaking through the exterior human shell…

After six days Jesus took Peter, James, and his brother John and led them up on a high mountain by themselves. He was transfigured in front of them, and his face shone like the sun; his clothes became as white as the light.

✡ *Matthew 17:1-2*

Imagine walking with the Lord and getting to know him personally. Imagine eating with him, drinking with him, and following him from place to place, watching him work. Think how much you would learn! That is exactly what happened with his disciples. Then one fine day, for a brief moment, he revealed a side of himself more amazing than a normal human being. His eternal power and glory began to break through, visibly; he was transfigured.

As a follower of Yeshua, you will also shine like a star in this broken world, and in the one to come. Praise God today for the wonder work he is doing in your life!

JULY 28

When you have spent time with the Lord, it makes a difference. You may be in a hurry one day, and forget to pray as you walk out the door. You may find yourself rushed from one activity to another, always running behind. Make it a point to draw close to him today, so that you can confidently walk the path he has set before you now.

While he was still speaking, suddenly a bright cloud covered them, and a voice from the cloud said: "This is my beloved Son, with whom I am well-pleased. Listen to him!"

✡ *Matthew 17:5*

When Yeshua was 'transfigured' – the Greek term is *metamorphothe*, the same word used when a caterpillar changes into a butterfly – he became radiant, as Moses did when he came down from Mount Sinai. Also notice in the verse above that a "bright cloud" enveloped his disciples, the same presence of God's glory which appeared on Mount Sinai. Finally, note that this verse says the same thing the Lord instructed previously in Exodus 23:20, *"Listen to him!"* Such amazing connections!

How is God connecting the dots in your own life? Review this passage closely, and pray as he leads…

<u>JULY 29</u>

It is so important to give everything to God. Lay it all at the foot of the cross – the good and the bad – and allow Yeshua to settle your accounts by his grace. After you have taken time to rest before the Lord, consider this encouraging passage about Yeshua. Why do you think he wanted to be approachable?

When the disciples heard this, they fell facedown and were terrified. Jesus came up, touched them, and said, "Get up; don't be afraid." When they looked up they saw no one except Jesus alone.

✡ *Matthew 17:6-8*

Imagine again being present at the transfiguration of Yeshua, an event that echoes Mount Sinai. Just like the children of Israel, his disciples were terrified! But after the cloud is gone, and everything settles down, who is standing there, *alone*, like a dear friend?

JULY 30

After the fall of mankind, Adam and Eve were kicked out of the garden. The world was subject to a curse, and the first couple was sentenced to hard work, tears, and blood. But work itself *predated* the fall. Adam had a job tending to the Garden of Eden, and caring for the animals. God has also given you tasks, so that your own mind, hands, and efforts can be used to glorify him. Consider the notion that your work is sacred…

The gate of the courtyard is to have a 30-foot screen embroidered with blue, purple, and scarlet yarn, and finely spun linen. It is to have four posts and their four bases. All the posts around the courtyard are to be banded with silver and have silver hooks and bronze bases.

✡ *Exodus 27:16-17*

Artisans and craftsmen were employed on God's behalf, making beautiful furnishings for the tabernacle. Careful planning and attention went into every detail. Do you treat your own work in the same way?

The tasks God has placed before you are important; every job is important. Today, complete this prayer: "Dear Lord, help me to understand my work the way you understand it…"

JULY 31

With an ancient olive press there are several types of oil produced. The finest oil, which comes from the initial pressing, was used in service of the Temple. It was the only oil allowed in the sacred menorah. The secondary oils would be used for cooking, perfume, and common soap. Like anything else, olive pressing takes work, and so does worship…

"You are to command the Israelites to bring you pure oil from crushed olives for the light, in order to keep the lamp burning regularly."

✡ *Exodus 27:20*

You may not see your own work as an act of worship, but it ought to be. Likewise, you may not consider the worship of God to be 'work' in the strictest sense, but sometimes walking with God can take great effort. Consider: what does it take for you to keep your own spiritual lamp burning inside? You can trust God to sustain your inner lamp when life is tiring, but you must also keep oil in your lamp, and wait on the Lord!

Read the verse carefully again, very slowly, and allow the word of God to refresh your supply.

<u>AUGUST 1</u>

If you have chosen to follow Yeshua, he has also chosen you. Your walk is a long journey, but God takes care of you every minute of every day. He died for you on the cross, and paved the path for your ultimate redemption. What then are you called to do?

In the tent of meeting outside the curtain that is in front of the testimony, Aaron and his sons are to tend the lamp from evening until morning before the Lord. This is to be a permanent statute for the Israelites throughout their generations.

✡ *Exodus 27:21*

Notice Aaron and his sons were responsible for keeping the lamps burning around the clock. In the same way, your responsibility as a believer is full-time, from evening until morning, and all throughout the day. So if your flame is dying, go to Yeshua in prayer. He will lift you up! If someone you know is weary, help re-ignite the fire by encouraging them.

Today, you may feel tired, but give him thanks and praise anyway. You will find it easier to do once you make the effort to praise him.

AUGUST 2

One of the greatest things you can do with your life
is to worship God with your talents and gifts.
Remember, the Lord made you as you are today,
and his purpose for you is important, reaching
further than you may appreciate. In light of this
verse from Exodus, how might you worship God
with your own gifts, talents, and resources?

*You are to instruct all the skilled artisans, whom I
have filled with a spirit of wisdom, to make Aaron's
garments for consecrating him to serve me as
priest.*

✡ *Exodus 28:3*

Sometimes you may find yourself in a position to
do something great, for free. Even when times are
tight, God still calls us to participate in ministry.
What skills do you have that God can use to bless
others? Is there some wisdom God has given you
that might be a life-saver to somebody else?

The men in the verse above were called specifically
to bless the priest. What can you do, specifically, to
help a brother or sister in the Lord serve God even
better than they already do?

<u>AUGUST 3</u>

There is nothing we have that has not been given to us. All the world belongs to God, with no exception, and even our most prized possessions are on loan. After you have taken a few moments to fix your thoughts on the Lord, consider what the following verse teaches us about the positions we hold in life.

The holy garments that belong to Aaron are to belong to his sons after him, so that they can be anointed and ordained in them.

✡ *Exodus 29:29*

Someday, even Aaron would have to step down from his post. When he did, his priestly garments would go to another person, his successor in line. Those clothes were not really his to begin with, they belonged to God.

Is there some position, or seniority, which you have in life that must ultimately be passed on to another at some point? How well have you taken care of the sacred garments which you have worn? Today, ask the Lord to guide you in these things. Also understand that he is not done with you. When the time comes to pass your legacy on, pray that God would provide a worthy descendant, and that he or she would walk in the wisdom of Yeshua.

<u>AUGUST 4</u>

You have much to be grateful for, and it is time to re-fuel. Be still, and listen with your heart to what the Spirit has to say. There are times for quiet reflection, and solitude; and there are times for celebration and singing. When you are taking stock, consider what you might give in response to his great sacrifice for you.

Each person should do as he has decided in his heart — not reluctantly or out of compulsion, since God loves a cheerful giver.

✡ *2 Corinthians 9:7*

Do you worship God with your finances? If not, perhaps this is a good time to begin doing so. A good rule of thumb is to earn all you can, save all you can, and give all you can. There is no percentage, or hard rule about charity, other than the cheerfulness of the giver. Yeshua did not complain about the cross. How much more thankful ought we to be, when we are called to bless others?

Today, allow the Lord to re-shape your heart when it comes to time, money, and resources. All the earth belongs to him. Who better to trust?

Pray as follows: "Dear Lord, I offer you my…"

<u>AUGUST 5</u>

In all your travels, through every door you walk, what is it that matters most of all? If you are a follower of Yeshua, the answer is simple but difficult: Love. Are there loved ones in your life who are not so easy to love? If we are honest, none of us are easy to love all the time! And yet, we are told in the Bible over and over to *love*. But what happens when it becomes painful? What happens when someone hurts us, so that we need to protect ourselves? Here is the answer…

Let brotherly love continue.

✡ *Hebrews 13:1*

You may have friends or family members who are unsafe. If so, it is important to protect yourself and others. In fact, that's the *loving* thing to do. We are told to love our enemies, but if we cannot love other believers as brothers and sisters, how can we even begin to love our enemies?

Pray about this today, something along these lines: "Dear Lord, if there is someone I ought to love, but have failed to, please show me…"

AUGUST 6

There is a raging spiritual battle all around us, every day, and it is largely unseen. In the heavenly realms there are multitudes of angels and demons warring for supremacy, and evil spirits prey upon the vulnerable souls of men and women. If you are a follower of Yeshua, you can be sure that, from the moment you were baptized, you stepped into a spiritual war. But take heart! The victory belongs to the Lord, and you are covered in the blood of Yeshua. In light of that reality, consider how you might treat others…

Don't neglect to show hospitality, for by doing this some have welcomed angels as guests without knowing it.

✡ *Hebrews 13:2*

It is unfortunate when people get fixated on demons and devils. There is no need for fear, if you have asked Yeshua into your heart. Nothing in the Bible teaches us to cast out specific demons, which rule over specific places. Instead, we are told to stand firm in the love of Yeshua. When you show hospitality to strangers, you are doing exactly that.

AUGUST 7

Do you find it difficult to empathize with people in hard situations? If so, turn off the videos, put aside the gadgets, and re-humanize yourself. Take a walk outside, breathe the clean air, and ask God to re-fill your heart. It is important that you stay in touch with the fact that you are a human being, created in God's image, and that other people matter to him as well.

Remember those in prison, as though you were in prison with them, and the mistreated, as though you yourselves were suffering bodily.

✡ *Hebrews 13:3*

Pray about an opportunity to step out of your own comfort zone. Are there things which you ought to do, but are afraid to do them because of how you might look? Yeshua entered into the dirt of mankind, and got bloodied for it. He could have protected himself from all of that, and stayed clean, but he set a better example for us to follow.

Complete this prayer today on your own: "Dear Lord, I was a prisoner before you rescued me. How might I step out and connect with someone in trouble today....?"

__AUGUST 8__

In our day *marriage* is under attack. This is not a political statement, it is a spiritual reality. Since the dawn of creation, the first couple in the Garden of Eden were subject to fierce spiritual attack, designed to tear them both apart. We may debate what marriage is, but in the eyes of God, it remains what it has always been: A lifetime covenant between a man, and a woman, with God holding it together. That is why the writer of Hebrews reminds us of the following.

Marriage is to be honored by all and the marriage bed kept undefiled, because God will judge the sexually immoral and adulterers.

✡ *Hebrews 13:4*

Make no mistake: God loves people in a profound way, but that is exactly why there will come a Day of Judgment. The evils of mankind can only continue for so long, until God will no longer allow it. To be sure, he is in no hurry to pour out wrath upon the heads of sinners, because he loves people enough to give second chances, and thirds, and fourths. But someday there will be an end to all sin, including adultery.

He is committed to you, so pray today, asking God to make your heart faithful to him. If you need to confess your sins to God, there is no better time than the present.

AUGUST 9

There is nothing in the world that you could ever need, which the Lord cannot provide. The most valuable gift he has given you is his grace, through Yeshua. In light of that great sacrifice and victory, the Bible encourages us to rest easy when it comes to material goods and worldly wealth…

Keep your life free from the love of money. Be satisfied with what you have, for he himself has said, I will never leave you or abandon you.

✡ *Hebrews 13:5*

If you put your trust in God, there is no amount of money which can ever buy you off. His faithfulness is worth more than gold. The Lord asks us to wait patiently, fixing our hearts on him, and trusting all the while that he knows everything we are going through, and that he cares about our future. Do not love money, love the Lord instead!

As you pray today, allow his promises to sink deep into your thoughts. Let this reality shape who you are: 'Never will I leave you; never will I forsake you!'

<u>AUGUST 10</u>

When it's dark outside, and chaos encroaches on your heart, reach out to Yeshua. When the earth shakes, call out to him. If you find yourself in a terror, he will hold you fast. You will be able to look back and recall with great comfort that he was there for you, that he pulled you through, and that the name of Yeshua was the first name on your lips when trouble came your way.

Therefore, we may boldly say, The Lord is my helper; I will not be afraid. What can man do to me?

✡ *Hebrews 13:6*

The answer to this question above is, nothing really. Man can harm your body, even kill you, but God can resurrect bodies. Man can attack your integrity, but God can look at you and say, "Well done, my good and faithful servant." Man can steal from you, but God can bring you into his Kingdom and give you new life.

Allow the Lord to guide you in prayer today. Let his truth be your guiding light.

<u>AUGUST 11</u>

Rest a moment before Yeshua. Take a deep breath, close your eyes, and allow the Holy Spirit to fill you. God is doing a great work in your life. Even though you may feel lost sometimes, he is ever present, working inside you very deeply. You might even say he is turning you into a great work of art.

You show that you are Christ's letter, delivered by us, not written with ink but with the Spirit of the living God — not on tablets of stone but on tablets of human hearts.

✡ *2 Corinthians 3:3*

The Greek word for 'letter' is *poema* – the same place we get our word *poem* from. Paul writes to the believing world, calling us a *poem* from the Messiah. But take note – our lives are being penned by the Spirit of God, not by handwriting, or stone carving. We are living a script which is being authored by God, etched into our hearts.

Today, ask the Lord to show you how your personal story should be lived out, to his glory.

<u>AUGUST 12</u>

You can serve God in a multitude of ways. Are you hospitable? Are you encouraging? Do you have a talent for helping others? All of these are paths by which you can worship God, and minister to people. In Yeshua, you have the best model to follow.

He has made us competent to be ministers of a new covenant, not of the letter, but of the Spirit. For the letter kills, but the Spirit gives life.

✡ *2 Corinthians 3:6*

The only time you have to worry about being in God's will, is when you are sinning. If you are sinning, you are not in his will. Apart from that, the Holy Spirit will always guide you with righteousness. You do not have to worry about being trained, or educated. You need only to trust the Holy Spirit to guide you with wisdom. Pray today for that wisdom!

You are on a mission which only you can complete. His Spirit will enable you to walk the road of eternal life, as a competent minister of the new covenant. Tell him everything in your heart.

AUGUST 13

We live in the best time in human history. We can look back and see the crosswork of Yeshua, and know what it means for our future destiny. In the time of Moses, the children of Israel could not do that. They stand as our forerunners, and our examples to learn from. Consider the distance between yourself and those people of the original Exodus…

Now if the ministry that brought death, chiseled in letters on stones, came with glory, so that the Israelites were not able to gaze steadily at Moses's face because of its glory, which was set aside, how will the ministry of the Spirit not be more glorious?

✡ *2 Corinthians 3:7-8*

The point of this passage is that we really do have it good. The children of Israel were fortunate to be able to look directly at Moses, and see the residue of the glory of God upon him. Today we would love to see that. But to our great fortune, we have the benefit of being able to look back at the resurrection of Yeshua, and see a hope which nobody before him had seen as clearly.

We can look to the future, and trust that God's glory will cause all of us to shine brightly like the stars. With the Holy Spirit living inside you, you have a very bright future. The Lord's greatest workmanship is just up ahead!

AUGUST 14

There may be times when you feel like a failure. This is natural and normal. Our feelings can wax and wane with the seasons. But if we can take hold of the truths of God, our minds can be renewed, and a bigger understanding can surmount our fickle feelings. In light of the ministry of Yeshua – his death, burial, and resurrection – how ought we to conduct ourselves in this world?

Since, then, we have such a hope, we act with great boldness.

✡ *2 Corinthians 3:12*

We have something the dying world does not have; we have a divine *hope*. This brand of hope stems from the fact that God is personally writing our story. Remember – you are his work of art, his *poem*. God is carefully shaping you through the circumstances of your life, and transforming you from something rough and earthly, into something heavenly, glorious, and radiant. It may be hard to believe sometimes, but that is the truth of the Scripture.

Pray for humility today, as you step out boldly for Yeshua.

<u>AUGUST 15</u>

In Yeshua, you are free to be a true child of God.
Apart from him, a person is not truly free to be what
God intended. God is doing a work in your life, but
those people who do not put their faith in Yeshua
are not filled with the Spirit; they are enslaved to sin
and death. Praising God for your freedom in
Yeshua is the only right thing to do.

*Now the Lord is the Spirit, and where the Spirit of
the Lord is, there is freedom.*

✡ *2 Corinthians 3:17*

You may wonder, for what reason did God give you
freedom in Yeshua? The answer is in Galatians 5:1,
"It is for freedom that Yeshua has set us free." In
other words, he set you free for freedoms sake.
Simply put, God loves freedom and liberty, and he
wants you to experience it. He rescued the children
of Israel from slavery, and rescued you from sin
through Yeshua. He has given you freedom
because that is how he made you to be.

You may feel trapped, and you may feel tied up.
Pray today, asking God the following: "Dear Lord,
please show me the grand perspective on my life,
and set me free from…"

AUGUST 16

When you were an infant, you could not sit up, or walk, or speak. All of those things you had to learn. In time you learned to read, write, and think clearly. Isn't it peculiar, just when you learn to handle yourself well, your body starts to age and slow down? Thankfully God is doing a good work in you, to carry you beyond death…

We all, with unveiled faces, are looking as in a mirror at the glory of the Lord and are being transformed into the same image from glory to glory; this is from the Lord who is the Spirit.

✡ *2 Corinthians 3:18*

Through the ministry of Yeshua, the Holy Spirit lives inside you. He is changing and shaping your life, your attitudes, your thoughts, and your heart. Allow him to! Ask him to do so! With ever-increasing glory, you are becoming the masterpiece, the *poem*, God wants you to be.

Even though your outside is aging, your inside is *breaking out*, preparing you to enter the Kingdom of God. When he is finished, you will be well suited for existence in Heaven. Pray today for an awareness of his deeper work in your life.

<u>AUGUST 17</u>

With every step, you come closer to the ultimate destination of your life's journey. Today, make sure to clothe yourself in Yeshua, who will protect you. God will answer your prayers as you seek him, and will deliver you, unscathed, into his courts of praise when your days on earth are done.

So they came to Philip, who was from Bethsaida in Galilee, and requested of him, "Sir, we want to see Jesus."

✡*John 12:21*

This verse is inscribed on the pulpits of many churches, as a reminder to preachers that the people come to church each week to see only one person – Yeshua. It should remind us that our personal quest may take us into many places, but when you go homeward it is God who awaits you at the finish line. One day you will see *him*!

Pray that your life would show Yeshua to others around you. Ask God to show you Yeshua in places where you may not have noticed before.

AUGUST 18

The last test a person will face in life is the test of dying well. Only in the comforting arms of the Lord can we be consoled with a promise that death is not the end. As you pray today, take time to acknowledge your frailness and human limits before God, then trust him for the strength to live your days well, starting with this day.

Truly I tell you, unless a grain of wheat falls to the ground and dies, it remains by itself. But if it dies, it produces much fruit.

✡*John 12:24*

Here Yeshua is speaking of his own death, and it was not without a purpose. The death of Yeshua means we have life in his resurrection. If you are in a tough spot, know this: Sometimes God will rescue you, other times he will simply reassure you.

Today, pray that God would fill you with the Holy Spirit, and grant you a steady walk. You might begin with, "Loving Lord, I know my body is mortal, and weak, but you can make me…"

__AUGUST 19__

The world is a trap in some ways. On one hand, we get a great many things from the world that are good, like food, water, shelter, music. But our eyesight can fool us into thinking this world is a greater treasure, in its present state, than it really is. Prepare your heart for devotional time today by asking the Lord to help you see life through his eyes.

The one who loves his life will lose it, and the one who hates his life in this world will keep it for eternal life.

✡ *John 12:25*

As our best possible example to follow, Yeshua willingly let go of his earthly life in exchange for heavenly glory. He understood something we, in our humanness, all too easily fail to grasp: This life is a mere shadow compared to the life on high, which God wants to give us. God has a plan for you today, and it involves living for him.

One day you will have the opportunity to fully embrace the new life, and when you look back on today, you will wonder why you were ever hesitant for even a moment. Ask the Holy Spirit then to fill you, and to give you a heavenly perspective on things.

AUGUST 20

People are born with a selfish ambition to be the center of the world. Little babies who have loving parents have no reason to believe things should be any different! But as we grow in our walk of faith, it should become clearer in our minds that the model for righteous living involves being a servant, not a master. When we come to know Yeshua, only then can we understand the way in which we have seen things incorrectly.

If anyone serves me, he must follow me. Where I am, there my servant also will be. If anyone serves me, the Father will honor him.

✡ *John 12:26*

The highest post a person can attain is that of a servant of God. In the Kingdom economy, it is the *servants* who God lifts up. The more you can humble yourself, and the more willing you are to see this life as the temporary way-station that it is, the better prepared you will be when the day comes for you to embrace eternity with Yeshua.

God will honor your prayers when you ask him to show you places of service. In prayer today, ask the Lord to show you some new places to serve, and to refresh the old places you are so familiar with.

AUGUST 21

People sometimes say there is always time to change course, always time to correct your ways, and always a second chance. But that's not exactly true. At a certain point you will have finished your work here on earth, and there will be no going back. Some things you cannot do over again. Read this verse and consider how very important it is to live each and every hour for Yeshua.

Jesus answered, "The light will be with you only a little longer. Walk while you have the light so that darkness doesn't overtake you. The one who walks in darkness doesn't know where he's going.

✡ *John 12:35*

Time is a priceless precious gift. Eventually the hourglass will be empty, as is the case for everyone, and you will be thankful for having walked in the light!

Without Yeshua we are simply stumbling around in the darkness, bumping into furniture, without a clue as to what opportunities we are throwing away. Since you have the Lord of light in your life, pray today for even more illumination inside!

AUGUST 22

Probably the greatest result that comes from walking with Yeshua, and serving him, is that you begin to resemble his character. Eventually all the imitation takes hold, and you can begin to the the outline of the person he is transforming you into. Even as you age, he is cultivating something new within you. Trust him to do that work.

While you have the light, believe in the light so that you may become children of light." Jesus said this, then went away and hid from them.

✡ *John 12:36*

Light does not simply mean shining, it means *goodness* and something *heavenly*. In your faithwalk, God is making you more heavenly every day. You may not notice it, and you probably don't recognize it within yourself, but he is the heavenly light, and his Spirit is the light within you.

Pray today for strength, wisdom, patience, and loving-kindness. Also, ask the Lord to show you what you might ask on behalf of other people.

AUGUST 23

One of the most beautiful pictures in the Bible is of God walking in the cool of the day, through the Garden of Eden, with his friend Adam. Before the fall, the relationship between God and humanity was flawless and unbroken. Now through Yeshua, we have a new chance to walk very closely with God, a critical need for each person.

"Daughter Zion, shout for joy and be glad, for I am coming to dwell among you" — this is the Lord's declaration.

✡ *Zechariah 2:10*

Imagine the Lord coming over to your house for a meal. What kind of preparations would you become involved with? Would you dress differently? Would you clean the house better? Fortunately, in Yeshua, he is bringing the festivities to *you*, so you can trust him to take care of the details! Even still, best to pray today for a prepared heart, ready to do whatever he sets before you, as you await his inevitable return.

AUGUST 24

It is hard to believe, but one day there really will be peace on Earth. It will not come through political powers, or through social programs. Instead, it will come from God himself. Even though the world is shocked with chaos, God will bring it all together by his holy power.

"Many nations will join themselves to the Lord on that day and become my people. I will dwell among you, and you will know that the Lord of Armies has sent me to you."

✡ *Zechariah 2:11*

At the return of Yeshua there will be judgment, but there will also be reward. He will walk among his people again, and will be available to us all. You will meet brothers and sisters, friends from all over the world and throughout history, all grateful for what Yeshua has done for us. When you pray today, remember those who do not yet know the Savior, and are yet to be reached in remote places.

<u>AUGUST 25</u>

The Lord God is sovereign over all the earth. There is no single square inch which does not belong personally to him. Even still, he has chosen a certain small stretch of land to show particular honor to. Israel belongs to Yeshua, as a part of his inheritance.

The Lord will take possession of Judah as his portion in the Holy Land, and he will once again choose Jerusalem.

✡ *Zechariah 2:12*

Jerusalem is by far the most religiously contentious city in the world, and too many wars have been fought over it. But God will reclaim it, once and for all, never to be trampled on again by anyone.

Imagine a day with *no* awful news coming from the Middle East. In God's timing that will come to pass. On this day, pray for the peace of Jerusalem!

AUGUST 26

When someone important enters a room – perhaps a judge, or a queen, or a commanding officer in the military – people are expected to stand at attention, out of respect for, and deference to, the high office. The same is true of the Lord. When God arrives, all people are expected to stop what they are doing, and pay full attention. His authority and holiness cause people to fall on their faces in complete submission. Consider this verse…

Let all people be silent before the Lord, for from his holy dwelling he has roused himself.

✡ *Zechariah 2:13*

In the face of God's total power and majesty, every single person is commanded to become still. He is the King of Kings, and his actions compel people into humility. As subjects of the King, we are not under the threat of his wrath, but instead we are part of his household – friends of Yeshua.

In preparation for his coming, practicing stillness before him is a very wise practice. During your devotional time today, practice being still before your God.

<u>AUGUST 27</u>

Aggressive use of force governs the world we live in. Any good student of human history will recognize that. Power and manipulation are the ways of the world, and that will never change so long as humanity is charting its own path. But the strength of Yeshua did not come from his wielding of raw power. Rather, in an act of sacrificial love, he laid down his life, and submitted to the will of the Father in heaven.

So he answered me, "This is the word of the Lord to Zerubbabel: 'Not by strength or by might, but by my Spirit,' says the Lord of Armies."

✡ *Zechariah 4:6*

If you have struggled to win certain battles in life, maybe your fighting has been misdirected on occasion. Have you ever tried to use earthly power to win spiritual battles? This calls for deep prayer and soul searching: Ask for God's grace and wisdom, to recognize areas in your life that call for your surrender, rather than your continued struggle. Ask the Holy Spirit to sustain you through *his* power, so that you can rest in him, and ask for discernment to know which areas call for resistance, and which call for your submission. His Spirit will aid you.

AUGUST 28

Often times we can be ungrateful for the circumstances in which we find ourselves. Life really is not fair, and in fact, it is often cruel and difficult. We may dislike our jobs, our daily routines, our neighborhoods, even those people who are close to us. But somehow, when God is on the throne, he repairs our hearts, so that our life situations come into better perspective.

We give you thanks, Lord God, the Almighty, who is and who was, because you have taken your great power and have begun to reign.

✡ *Revelation 11:17*

Give thanks today, because God is still in charge. He always has been. Nobody else can lay claim to your life the way he does, and nobody else loves you so much. His kingdom is your reward, and through Yeshua you have a place there.

Praise God today as you prepare for what lies ahead, and allow him to give you the words to pray.

<u>AUGUST 29</u>

If the rat race has kicked you around lately, do not be afraid. The Lord is with you, he has a greater plan, and you are part of it. It is important that you make a decided effort to stay in communion with God, and take your devotional time seriously. You will not be sentenced to eternal drudgery when your days are through; you will be ushered into a sweet eternal Sabbath rest. With expectation in your heart, pray diligently, seek the face of Yeshua, and ask the Lord to protect you from sin.

But encourage each other daily, while it is still called today, so that none of you is hardened by sin's deception.

✡ *Hebrews 3:13*

Hopefully you have some friends and family members who are believers in Yeshua, like you are. And ideally you will all hold each other accountable when one of you slips up. Sometimes a firm warning is also a great encouragement! If there is someone in your circle who needs encouragement, be willing to be that person. Also, be willing to hear it from someone else. A wise person accepts correction, but a fool departs from wisdom.

AUGUST 30

If you have been walking with Yeshua for a long time, no doubt you have experienced seasons of intimacy, as well as feelings of being distant from God. It has been said by many preachers, if you feel distant from God, it's not because he went anywhere! Take a few moments to recall the circumstances under which you first came to faith in Yeshua. Was it a long time ago? Have you changed much since then? At the same time, consider how many challenges and struggles he has brought you through!

For we have become participants in Christ if we hold firmly until the end the reality that we had at the start.

✡ *Hebrews 3:14*

If a dear friend scheduled a lunch date with you two months from today, at a certain place, at a certain hour, but did not call you later to confirm the lunch, would you be able to trust that friend to be there when you arrived? A good friend will always keep his or her word. Likewise, Yeshua has placed his Holy Spirit within you, and the promise he made to you long ago still holds firm today.

You can count on him to be there as you run your race. Hold firm to him – he will always hold on to you.

<u>AUGUST 31</u>

Distractions abound in our busy world. But you don't have to let those things crowd out your spiritual life. In fact, it is important that you continue to return to Yeshua, and to times of deep prayer. Take time to settle in, close your eyes, and breathe deeply. The Lord loves you, he is with you, and always hears your prayers.

Therefore, since the promise to enter his rest remains, let us beware that none of you be found to have fallen short.

✡ *Hebrews 4:1*

If you have ever wondered if God has forgotten you, he has not. There is an eternal Sabbath waiting for you in his Kingdom. Do not lose heart! Even in your moments of greatest weakness, when everything feels aligned against you, plead with God to bring comfort to your heart.

Even if you are exhausted, you can be encouraged that he will carry you home. Pray today that God would strengthen you deep within, and help you to stand strong.

SEPTEMBER 1

When the Hebrews of old were wandering in the desert, there were many who decided the journey was too much. They gave up on God, and they felt disdain for Moses. They hardened their hearts! This stands as a negative example for us to learn from. Is your heart open to what God is doing in your life? Is there any bitterness in your heart toward someone who God has partnered you with? Now is the time to do business with Yeshua.

Today, if you hear his voice, do not harden your hearts.

✡ *Hebrews 4:7*

In your long race toward home, toward the Kingdom of God, you may be tripped up by obstacles you yourself have placed in your own path. A hardened heart can be one of those obstacles. Nobody can bring your heart to God but you.

Even if you have done it a thousand times, once again, tell the Lord you need him to soften your spirit. Not every hill is worth dying on, and this world is not your home anyway. Pray as the Lord leads you today. But as you sense him leading you, ask him to break your heart over the things that break his. It is better to shed tears than have a hardened heart.

SEPTEMBER 2

Isn't it funny how quickly the time flies? All the more reason to carve out some quiet time with Yeshua, and slow things down. The deeper life is the best life, and it allows you to become more sensitive to the Spirit. You may have questions or problems left unsettled, but those things can be given to the Lord, and you can trust him to work everything out. For now, consider the promise of this sweet verse, and the fellowship you have with your God…

Therefore, a Sabbath rest remains for God's people. For the person who has entered his rest has rested from his own works, just as God did from his.

✡ *Hebrews 4:9-10*

Did you ever stop to think that you have some good things in common with the Lord? That's because he made you in his image. God did not rest because he was tired, he rested because his work of creation was completed. In the same way, one day your earthly work will be all done, and you'll have a whole new life and adventure to live with him.

Draw comfort from the fact that God is guiding your life in a similar way to how he himself lives. There will be a Sabbath-rest for you, like never before. When you reach it, you will not collapse from fatigue, instead you will be rejuvenated with the holy power of his resurrection.

<u>SEPTEMBER 3</u>

God is calling you to him. Every day, every morning when you rise, he is drawing you ever closer. You are growing in your faith, and wisdom is your guidepost. The Lord is like a beacon on the shore, shining a bright light of hope for you to follow. Take some time to rest in the Lord. Go through the ritual you have set for yourself, and let him bring *shalom* into your heart.

Let us then make every effort to enter that rest, so that no one will fall into the same pattern of disobedience.

✡ *Hebrews 4:11*

As a child of God you are under the watchful eye of a divine parent. You may not know it, but he is constantly protecting you. When he directs you, it is best to obey, and come to him without hesitation. It may seem paradoxical that you have to make such a great effort to enter into a time of rest, but God is not calling you to be busy. He is calling you to *rest in him.*

Today, determine to finish well, do right by everybody, and enjoy the peace he gives to a restful heart.

<u>SEPTEMBER 4</u>

There is one, and only one, King and Ruler over the universe. Politicians come and go, and so do tyrants. But God rules the universe forever, and decides who will preside, and for how long. All power is on loan from God. Take some time today to consider the prophet Samuel, and how he reluctantly handed the reins of leadership over to a human king. The children of Israel asked for a king, and God granted their plea.

If you fear the Lord, worship and obey him, and if you don't rebel against the Lord's command, then both you and the king who reigns over you will follow the Lord your God.

✡ *1 Samuel 12:14*

Even the best leaders need to be in submission to God. No skill or talent can replace humility before Yeshua. Perhaps you are in a position of leadership yourself. If so, it is a blessing to serve and obey God. Everyone will be better for it. And if you have a leader above you who does not, then never fear. God alone holds power over the universe.

No earthly king or ruler intimidates God. Pray today for a healthy level of awe and respect for God's power, and his loving authority.

SEPTEMBER 5

When the children of Israel asked for a king, they did not expect to learn they had sinned. They simply thought it was a good to be like every other nation. But if you are under the direct governance of the Lord, there is no better place to be. When they learned better it was through God's mercy, not his wrath. He allowed them to have a king, but also showed them a mighty display of his own power, which no earthly ruler could ever match…

Samuel called on the Lord, and on that day the Lord sent thunder and rain. As a result, all the people greatly feared the Lord and Samuel.

✡ *1 Samuel 12:18*

Maybe your country is not in submission to Yeshua, but you can be. Take time to do what Yeshua suggested: Look at the birds, consider the flowers. Really look at life. God tends to these things without their awareness. In the same way, he cares for you continually.

If you have sinned, God is desirous of bringing you back to right standing. Through Yeshua you are set right. Today, ask the Lord to teach you through grace and mercy, so that you might learn things without having to do everything the hard way.

SEPTEMBER 6

One of the most important lessons we learn from Samuel is, never give up! God is not done with you, even if you've hit rock bottom. No matter what life throws at you, do not lose heart, because you have a risen Savior on your side, and he will not let you down.

Samuel replied, "Don't be afraid. Even though you have committed all this evil, don't turn away from following the Lord. Instead, worship the Lord with all your heart.

✡ *1 Samuel 12:20*

Sometimes it may seem like we have run our race, and lost. We feel disqualified. But if you have breath in lungs today, take the words of Samuel to heart: "Do not be afraid…serve the Lord with all your heart!"

You may not get the chance to live your past over again, but you can give *this* day to Yeshua, and rest in his promise to redeem you. In him you can walk humbly, with strength, and in full confidence that your finish line will be in his kingdom. Ask him to be with you now, and in today's travels.

SEPTEMBER 7

The source for all joy and contentment is actually pretty simple: Trust in Yeshua. That's really all it comes down to. All the self-help books in the world do not add up when compared to him. At the end of the day, if you hold onto any singular thing in the world, hold on tightly to Yeshua. Consider the wisdom of the prophet Samuel…

Don't turn away to follow worthless things that can't profit or rescue you; they are worthless.

✡ *1 Samuel 12:21*

There is no item, object, or relationship which can deliver you from the curse of death, other than Yeshua. Through his crosswork, you are given the chance to have new life, eternal life, bursting out from the grave. He will give you a new body, a new heart, and a new understanding. Earthly possessions can do you no good, because they cannot rescue you the way Yeshua can. He is the only divine lifeguard in the universe.

Today, close your eyes, breathe deeply, and allow the Holy Spirit to make you aware of your surroundings. Nothing you wear, eat, or sit on is permanent. But your faith in Yeshua is for ever after.

SEPTEMBER 8

Isn't it good to know that you have a God who loves you? Unlike all those false gods that people fabricate, you have a real, living, loving heavenly Father, who guides you even when you aren't thinking about it. God has made plenty of great promises to his people, which should keep you encouraged until the end of your days. He looked at you, felt compassion in his heart for you, and decided to make you his child.

The Lord will not abandon his people, because of his great name and because he has determined to make you his own people.

✡ *1 Samuel 12:22*

As a follower of Yeshua you have marvelous things in store. You are a part of the people of God! And as one of his people, he will never reject you, even when you blow it from time to time.

Though the death, burial, and resurrection of Yeshua must have been painful for God the Father to watch, it makes him happy to see you reconciled to him. He wanted you back where you belong, in the fold of God, and at home in the heavenly realm of Yeshua. Today, pray along these lines: "Dear Lord, I want to submit to you in a new way. Help me to honor your name today in the following areas…"

SEPTEMBER 9

If you have had some friction recently – and who has not? – it may be a good time for you to lay it at the foot of the cross. Sometimes even our favorite people can rub us the wrong way; it's a part of being human. Take stock of your life, and remember the moments when you may have been less than humble, less than patient, and less than loving. If you have something to say to someone, consider how you might make amends. In the meantime, pray for a person who really needs it, as Samuel did for the nation…

As for me, I vow that I will not sin against the Lord by ceasing to pray for you. I will teach you the good and right way.

✡ *1 Samuel 12:23*

Samuel prayed for the children of Israel, even after they had sinned. In fact, he saw it as sinful to neglect prayer! You can take comfort in the fact that you may pray to God as often as you are able, and he hears your heart even when you do not intentionally pray.

If you pray with words today, take the time to share with him your concerns. He is happy to hear you.

SEPTEMBER 10

Allow the Lord to settle your heart, to calm your mind, and to focus your attention on his holiness. There is only one God, and he wants to show you new dimensions of his glory, and his plan for you today. Consider the profound implications of Yeshua's words to Nicodemus, the man who was called to be Israel's teacher…

If I have told you about earthly things and you don't believe, how will you believe if I tell you about heavenly things?

✡ *John 3:12*

As earthly people, it can be very easy for us to think of the world only in terms of what we can see with our eyes. But the Bible teaches, and Yeshua affirms, that the heavenly realms beyond the visible eye, and beyond the range of our most powerful telescopes, are filled with the presence of God. In reality, our concrete physical world is only one aspect of the universe God rules over.

In light of this difficult to imagine truth, pray today for a perspective that transcends this world. Ask God to show you glimpses of eternity in the ordinary things around you. Start by praying, "Dear Lord, please open my eyes to see you in…"

SEPTEMBER 11

Have you ever had a friend who took a long trip to somewhere remote and exotic? Maybe you yourself have gone on a mission trip to someplace very different. When you meet someone who has been to places foreign to you, do you find it intriguing to hear about aspects of life in other parts of the world? If so, consider what Yeshua has to say about the kingdom of heaven…

No one has ascended into heaven except the one who descended from heaven — the Son of Man.

✡ *John 3:13*

If the Bible paints an accurate picture of Yeshua, then he is a first class traveler with passport stamps we ordinary human beings can only dream of. He spoke of heaven as if it were real, tangible, local, and accessible. He also told us how even we might get there, namely, through faith in him. He is the eternal Son of God, and only he can accurately report what heaven is like.

In prayer today, begin by expressing to the Lord your own longing for a better place, but also your willingness to wait, and to walk by faith.

SEPTEMBER 12

Every apparent accident of history is sovereignly superintended by God; even the disasters and the tragedies. There is no question that the Lord is good, and he hates evil, yet the worst human rebellion is not outside of his control. Like a good father, he can discipline humanity with compassionate strength. Think on this timeless verse…

Just as Moses lifted up the snake in the wilderness, so the Son of Man must be lifted up, so that everyone who believes in him may have eternal life.

✡ *John 3:14-15*

Out in the desert the children of Israel were rebelling. God sent poisonous snakes in response. But in his mercy, he allowed for a 'cure' in the hand-carved snake Moses lifted up over his head. In the same way, if you look to Yeshua, the cure for your sin will be administered. Sin is like an extreme poison, racing through your bloodstream to kill you. But if you simply look to Yeshua in faith, that will rescue you, and heal your dire state.

Recommit your life to him today. "Loving Heavenly Father, again I place myself in your hands…"

SEPTEMBER 13

Probably the best known verse in the Bible is John 3:16. But interestingly, there is a question as to who actually makes this great statement. Is it Yeshua himself speaking? Or is it John explaining the reasoning behind the great sacrifice of the Messiah? Even though the red-letter Bibles attribute these words to Yeshua, it may be that John is the one saying them, as he tries to explain *why* God was willing to give his only begotten Son…

For God loved the world in this way: He gave his one and only Son, so that everyone who believes in him will not perish but have eternal life.

✡ *John 3:16*

The meaning of the verse is wonderfully simple: God has given Yeshua as a sacrifice for us, so that we too could have eternal life after death. Why? Because God loves the world even though it is fallen and sinful. He loved the world enough to give his own Son for us. This is the greatest act of selfless love the world has ever known.

To be sure, no matter who said it, God himself has made certain that the truth of this verse would found its way down to you today. Pray over it, embrace it, walk in it, and live thankfully, knowing that the Lord has thought of everything, even the problem of death.

Begin your prayers with, "Dear God, I thank you for the gift of your Son. And I freely give you…"

SEPTEMBER 14

Going deeper with Yeshua is a good thing. Some truths which seem to be clearly simple often lead to bigger questions, and new opportunities to marvel at the majesty of God's love and wisdom. If you have ever looked around and wondered about the pain and difficulty of life, wishing you could understand the motives of God, look no further than this verse…

For God did not send his Son into the world to condemn the world, but to save the world through him.

✡*John 3:17*

The Lord knows about your suffering, and he knows about your fears. He is not gleefully causing you to hurt, or ignoring you. In fact, he shares your tears.

God's desire is not to send people to hell, but to rescue us into heaven. He is not, like so many of us, impatiently wanting to see evil people destroyed. Quite the opposite, he is giving the world as much time as humanity needs to come to repentance. He came with a mind to save, not to condemn.

Pray for God's peace, as you step out into your day. You will need it when you encounter the normal evils of the world, as they put pressure on you.

SEPTEMBER 15

Standing alongside the loving patience of God is also his holy and unshakable commitment to divine justice. Even though God loves the world, and would much rather save it into heaven, there will come a certain Day when the Lord will say enough is enough. He has sent Yeshua, and there is no other path to salvation. Death and evil will be burnt up in a quick instant.

Anyone who believes in him is not condemned, but anyone who does not believe is already condemned, because he has not believed in the name of the one and only Son of God.

✡ *John 3:18*

As the Son of God, Yeshua represents the exact form and reality of God the Father. He is the only Son of God, and the only road to life. Ask God for wisdom in your prayers today. Let your rest in him be a joy, and a chance to refuel. Your life's mission is still ongoing!

SEPTEMBER 16

Everyone needs help seeing the way forward. If you were an actual *sheep*, you would need a shepherd to guide you, and direct you everywhere you went. You wouldn't have any idea where the best grass was, or where to get water from, or how to find your way home. Spiritually speaking, that is how all people really are. We need the Lord to protect us from danger and even from ourselves. Here is a prayer from Moses which was answered in the coming of Yeshua…

May the Lord, the God who gives breath to all, appoint a man over the community who will go out before them and come back in before them, and who will bring them out and bring them in, so that the Lord's community won't be like sheep without a shepherd.

✡ *Numbers 27:16-17*

In Mark 6:34, we are told that Yeshua had compassion on the people around him because they were like "sheep without a shepherd." He saw that they needed spiritual food, as well as something to eat. If you are in need today, ask the good shepherd to lead you. Moses knew his people would be lost without the guidance of a good shepherd, and Yeshua has filled that role perfectly, leading the way into the kingdom of heaven.

SEPTEMBER 17

If you ever thought you were nothing special, it would bless you to know the way God sees you. As you settle into your devotional time today, give thanks to the Lord for the simple things: health, food, your friends. If you have a heavy heart, ask him to help you walk the faithwalk today. He knows you better than you may think, and he is well aware of the fact that you need his sustaining love in your life today.

I chose you before I formed you in the womb; I set you apart before you were born.

✡ *Jeremiah 1:5*

In the eyes of Yeshua you are no accident. You may not be everything you wish to be, but he is leading you into something greater than your wildest dreams. He knew what you would become before you were even conceived.

Trust him today with all your concerns, and take heart. The path you walk is the one Yeshua tread many years ago, and he has shown you the way forward from here – walking by faith, trusting in him.

SEPTEMBER 18

If you have walked with Yeshua for any amount of time, you will encounter those who hold him in disdain. What can you do when people despise your faith? Jeremiah the prophet had these same fears, and God told him the following…

Do not be afraid of anyone, for I will be with you to rescue you. This is the Lord's declaration.

✡ *Jeremiah 1:8*

It may be that you feel isolated and alone, but he has not forgotten or abandoned you. The work he has for you is not done until he calls you home, and when you run into problems or even persecution, you can trust in his promise to rescue you. He will deliver you from your enemies, from sin, and eventually from death. You will look back on all your fears one day, and laugh with joy, understanding how much he truly loves you.

Pray today for his strength, for direction, and anything else he puts on your heart. He is always wanting to hear your prayers!

SEPTEMBER 19

Another new day! A chance to start over with a clean slate. The mercies of God are new every morning! Even still, maybe you are feeling stretched, tired, and run down. Nevertheless, the Lord is strong when you are weak, and if you put your trust in him once again, he will carry you through the storms. Take a moment and relax your thoughts, as you enter into a time of devotion and prayer. You are not the first person to tread the path you are on!

By faith Abraham, when he was called, obeyed and set out for a place that he was going to receive as an inheritance. He went out, even though he did not know where he was going.

✡ *Hebrews 11:8*

Do you know, for certain, where you are going? All believers in Yeshua share a hope for the future, a final destination which will be a glorious, rewarding relief. But what will it look like, your Promised Land? You don't know. And in that respect you are just like Abraham – an adventurer on a quest. Only God knows what your destination will look like, but you can certainly trust him to get you there!

Continue this prayer: "Dear God, I want my life to be an adventure of faith, please take me wherever you will…"

SEPTEMBER 20

Sometimes discipline can seem like hatred, when we are going through painful times. You may have done nothing wrong, yet God allows you to experience some very rough patches. If that is the case today, consider the relationship the Lord has with Israel as a people. Why would God allow his beloved to be harmed? Why would he allow us to walk through the valley of the shadow of death? And what happens when God seems to turn his back on his own?

Israel was holy to the Lord, the firstfruits of his harvest. All who ate of it found themselves guilty; disaster came on them." This is the Lord's declaration.

✡ *Jeremiah 2:3*

The reasoning of God is sometimes far out of the reach of mankind. Looking back on the fall of Jerusalem during the time of Jeremiah, one would never have guessed that God was clearing the path for the coming Messiah. All hope seemed lost, and God had apparently turned his back on his children. But we can trust his goodness, and his character.

One day, once again, Israel will stand holy before him. And his people will be renewed as the first-fruits of resurrection from the dead. Is it worth it today, to trust him with all things? YES!

SEPTEMBER 21

There is no question that God desires his people to be holy. God would go to unending lengths to purify his people, in order to restore the relationship he desires to have with his own children, including you. He would move mountains, fill oceans, and even give his own life for the sake of *your* holiness.

And his disciples remembered that it is written:
Zeal for your house will consume me.

✡ *John 2:17*

In this verse from the gospel of John, the passage his disciples remembered comes from Psalm 69:9. John uses it in reference to Yeshua driving out money changers from the holy temple.

If you are willing to follow him, he will go to any extreme in order to drive the sin away from your life. You will not see perfection on this side of the grave, but you can trust him to clean house entirely, and give you a purified heart, and eternal life. What could be better than that? Approach your God with an open heart today. There is nothing he wouldn't do for you.

SEPTEMBER 22

Take some time to settle your thoughts before the Lord. Allow the Holy Spirit to fill your heart and prepare you to receive God's word. The times you spend with him are precious, and help you face the challenges of the day. He loves you, he cares for you, and is committed to your protection and spiritual growth. Your life is a gift! How then will you respond the next time things become difficult? Read, and re-read this verse…

What is the source of wars and fights among you? Don't they come from your passions that wage war within you?

✡ *James 4:1*

Yeshua took all our sins upon himself when he went to the cross. You do not need to worry about your final destiny – God will take you there. But in the meantime, there is still the daily struggle between your sin nature, and the Spirit who lives within you.

Today in prayer, ask God to help you overcome the impulse to have everything your way. He will not only help you with this, in time he will make it easier, and you will be happier.

SEPTEMBER 23

God made you a *'sensate'* being. In other words, he gave you senses so that you could interact with the world around you. You were meant to taste, smell, touch, see, and hear. But your very *heart* is a sensing organ as well, and it can be lured into falling in love with the world around you. Consider this passage...

Don't you know that friendship with the world is hostility toward God? So whoever wants to be the friend of the world becomes the enemy of God. Or do you think it's without reason that the Scripture says: The spirit he made to dwell in us envies intensely? But he gives greater grace. Therefore he says: God resists the proud, but gives grace to the humble.

✡ *James 4:4-6*

Even though God has given you senses and needs, he personally desires your 100% devotion. Thankfully, as the text says, he gives us grace! If not for his merciful grace, we would be forever entangled in love with this world. By giving his son, Yeshua, as a sacrifice, he has provided a way for you to decisively become a friend of God.

SEPTEMBER 24

The reason it is so very important to spend quiet time with the Lord, is because your days are filled with conflict and spiritual war. You may not be aware of it all the time, and unfortunately people often wait to come to God until they are in acute pain, but there is a war being waged for your soul. How do you prepare for battle? Through prayer! Thank God he is ever present for you, because this may be a rough day.

Therefore, submit to God. Resist the devil, and he will flee from you.

✡ *James 4:7*

In your faithwalk, you will always have choices to make. Sometimes the choice is clear, and sometimes not. When you are in the middle of a spiritual battle, the enemy of your soul will try to temp you into rationalizing a bad choice. This verse from James is directly applicable then: Resist! If you can send out even the most desperate prayer to God, do so!

In moments of weakness, once you allow the Lord to govern your actions, resisting sin will become possible. And even though you will struggle against temptation your entire earthly life, one day the devil will flee from you *permanently*. Isn't that worth rejoicing over? Tell Yeshua about it in prayer today!

SEPTEMBER 25

Back in the Garden of Eden, mankind was given an enormous amount of freedom. They could eat from any tree they wanted to, with only one exception. Today, even though we are no longer sinless because of the fall from grace, we can actively cooperate in our own restoration by accepting Yeshua's death as our atoning sacrifice. To do so, we must continually return to him with a humble heart, and ask for grace and forgiveness. By doing so, you will naturally cultivate an intimate relationship with your loving Heavenly Father. Read this verse and ponder deeply what it means.

Draw near to God, and he will draw near to you. Cleanse your hands, sinners, and purify your hearts, you double-minded.

✡ *James 4:8*

One promise you can hold onto, is that God will respond to your intentions. If your heart seeks him, he will draw near to you in love. He sees you as a child lost in the woods, wandering about, looking to find your way home. Your home is with him, and he is ready to lead you there.

As for this day, is there any area in your life in which you have been double-minded, or unclean? Are there things you need to repent of? You know what those things are, deep down inside. Do not deny it, or hesitate to confess it to him today in prayer. He will honor your honesty.

SEPTEMBER 26

Proverbs teaches, there is a way that seems right to a man, but it leads to destruction. If you read your Bible carefully, you will find God's word is not too kind to the thoughts and philosophies of men. Even the greatest human thinkers are small compared to God. Yet, we are called to reason our way through the Scripture, using the brains God has given us. Since that is the case, we must wrestle with verses like this one, which seem to fly in the face of all human logic…

Humble yourselves before the Lord, and he will exalt you.

✡ *James 4:10*

Paradoxically, if you do not aggressively seek power and influence, but instead consider yourself fortunate to even be alive, God will "lift you up." Similarly, if you serve others, those less fortunate than yourself, God will reward your effort and crown you as his *servant*. In the Kingdom of God, to be a *humble servant* is the best job you can apply for.

Yeshua was just such a servant. He condescended, bent his desires, and submitted to a dreadful earthly death in order to serve *you*. Because of this, he has been lifted up, and so may you be too. Today pray that your heart would be humble before the Lord, so that he can show you off to the cosmos.

SEPTEMBER 27

One thing you can count on every day, for the rest of your life and beyond, is the word of God. His promises are rock solid. It is easy to become distressed by the overwhelming ruckus which is our fallen world, but God has pledged to restore and recreate all things, including even you. Because of that, the temporal nature of our lives is nothing to be concerned about, though we are wise to ponder our own mortality. Consider this beautiful verse, and the promise it provides.

The grass withers, the flowers fade when the breath of the Lord blows on them; indeed, the people are grass. The grass withers, the flowers fade, but the word of our God remains forever.

✡ *Isaiah 40:7-8*

Even though we all come to an end, God will not forsake us to the grave. Yeshua has died and risen again! As brief as our lives are, there is an eternity waiting for us in heaven, which will far outshine this present life. Let your heart take solace in his enduring word, as you reach out to him in prayer today.

SEPTEMBER 28

Change is a normal part of life. Some changes come abruptly and catch us off guard, while others occur slowly over time. Take time to reflect, and consider what God has been leading you to do. Are you on the precipice of a major change? Perhaps there are things you need to finally, once and for all, get around to taking care of. Either way, you can trust your Heavenly Father to see you through, and take you down the right path.

The Lord our God spoke to us at Horeb: 'You have stayed at this mountain long enough.'

✡ *Deuteronomy 1:6*

At a certain point all things give way to the heavy hand of *time*. No human activity or occupation is forever. Some things fall into our hands, while others are removed, and over time we see that people really are like temporary flowers in the fields.

Make the most of your days, starting today, by praying that Yeshua would fill you with the Holy Spirit. Also, ask him to give you the wisdom to see which mountains you may need to climb down from, and which one to climb up next.

SEPTEMBER 29

In every great story there is a time for action. Your story is the same way. At some point you will need to stand up, focus, and go do just what God is calling you to do. It may be that you feel small and insignificant at times, but that is not the reality: Everyone is important, and every calling is important too. You must simply find the courage.

See, the Lord your God has set the land before you. Go up and take possession of it as the Lord, the God of your fathers, has told you. Do not be afraid or discouraged.

✡ *Deuteronomy 1:21*

You have a responsibility before God to take care of the business only you can tend to. You have relationships, obligations, and areas of life which he has set before *you*, and nothing should keep you from doing your part.

Is there someone or something you need to protect? Are you duty bound to a certain ministry? Think on these things, and ask Yeshua to show you the proverbial *land* he wants you to take possession of. When you are prayerful, he will most certainly walk with you.

<u>SEPTEMBER 30</u>

God is our mighty king, and our protective shelter. He looks after you in a way that no parent, police officer, or president ever could. The Lord is looking after your soul. Fortunately for us, he is the strongest being in the universe, and he is entirely good.

See, the Lord God comes with strength, and his power establishes his rule. His wages are with him, and his reward accompanies him. He protects his flock like a shepherd; he gathers the lambs in his arms and carries them in the fold of his garment. He gently leads those that are nursing.

✡ *Isaiah 40:10-11*

If you are concerned about the future, put your trust in the Good Shepherd – Yeshua. He has blazed the trail, and will usher you into his rest. Take comfort in the knowledge that you are close to his heart at all times. Nothing in all creation can take you away from him.

Your Lord has plans for you, and also a reward, for the faith you have placed in him. Express your gratitude to Yeshua today; ask him to fill you with his Spirit, and teach you how to live!

__OCTOBER. 1__

Once in a while, each and every one of us really messes up. Can you relate? As a simple person with feet made of clay, there will certainly come times when you miss a golden opportunity, or make the wrong choice, or simply not do what you ought to have done. If that's something you can identify with, join the club. The children of Israel made grave mistakes, then went back and tried to correct them after it was too late. Consider the words of Moses…

You answered me, 'We have sinned against the Lord. We will go up and fight just as the Lord our God commanded us.' Then each of you put on his weapons of war and thought it would be easy to go up into the hill country.

✡ *Deuteronomy 1:41*

After missing your own proverbial boat, it is important to stop and learn the bigger lesson. If God has called you to do something, you only have one lifetime to get it done! Your time is precious. Don't make the mistake of living wrong, when you can live the right way today. If you don't move forward, then you may find that your next attempt will be like the Israelites trying to go unprepared into battle, after they had already blown their first chance.   If that sounds like you, stop, repent, and learn the full lesson now!

<u>OCTOBER. 2</u>

In the book of Acts, we meet a man named Stephen, who became the first martyr of the fledgling Christian church; it was his calling from God. Bravely, he stood up and spoke the truth in the face of violent hostility. As a result, he was killed by people who hated the good message of Yeshua. But in his last speech, the greatest of his life, he quoted the prophet Isaiah…

Heaven is my throne, and the earth my footstool. What sort of house will you build for me?

✡ *Acts 7:49*

Mankind has always tried to reduce God to fit our small estimation. But God has created everything, and he desires a humble heart in each of us. Our biggest ideas may not look anything like his divine plans – but no matter. He will have his way in the universe, because he is our Creator. Fortunately, that takes all the pressure off of us!

Submit your plans to Yeshua today, and allow him to redirect your life in any way he chooses.

__OCTOBER. 3__

As the seasons change, make sure you invite God into your heart regularly. You do not need to travel far to meet him; he is there before your pray even a single word. Allow his peace to fill you.

When they heard these things, they were enraged and gnashed their teeth at him. Stephen, full of the Holy Spirit, gazed into heaven. He saw the glory of God, and Jesus standing at the right hand of God.

✡ *Acts 7:54-55*

Have you ever considered the reception which awaits you when you take your final step into the arms of Yeshua? He will receive you like a long lost relative in a joyful reunion after many long years. Your life may be difficult, and your end may even be frightening, but all of that will fade away when you see him face to face. He is the best friend you could have in the entire universe. Ask him to come alongside and accompany you today, and he *will*.

<u>OCTOBER. 4</u>

What a world we live in! Soaked in sin, shocked with turmoil, and steeped in pain – yet so beautiful too. We all need Yeshua now more than ever, and prayer is the pathway to intimacy with God. Close your eyes and breathe deeply, allowing the Holy Spirit to sweep away the clutter and noise from your thoughts. No need to worry, it will all still be there when you are finished with your devotional time. But for a few moments, get closer to the Lord, and allow him to minister to you. Consider this short but powerful verse…

"Comfort, comfort my people," says your God.

✡ *Isaiah 40:1*

When your mind is reeling from stress, and your heart is heavy with fear about the future, remember to take comfort from the Lord. You are one of his people if you trust in Yeshua, so there is a mighty hope for you. He is more powerful than all the insanity of the world, so you have a strong and solid rock to stand on.

Today, pray that Yeshua would minister to you: "Dear Lord, please help me to rest in you. Take my…"

OCTOBER. 5

Nothing on Earth escapes the gaze of Almighty God. There is no sin, no lie, no corruption, and no evil human deed which slips by him. At the same time, he also sees the smallest acts of kindness. In the end, those selfless deeds will be part of the reward he gives to you. All accounts will be settled, and those who trust in Yeshua, and walk by faith, will be generously blessed.

And the glory of the Lord will appear, and all humanity together will see it, for the mouth of the Lord has spoken.

✡ *Isaiah 40:5*

You can count on God to keep his word in the Scriptures. And when Isaiah the prophet tells us specifically that all humanity will see the glory of the Lord, you can bank on it. For many, this will be an awful day of wrath, but for the children of God, it will be the greatest relief.

Pray now that Yeshua would help you to see ways in which you can touch other people's lives for the sake of the Kingdom. "Dear Lord, I want to lift up the following people to you today…"

<u>OCTOBER. 6</u>

What sort of battles do you fight? Do you have ambitions? Goals? Maybe you are heavily involved in political issues, or matters of power and money. Or perhaps your biggest battle is with your own physical body, or with a family member. Whatever the case may be, take a few minutes to sit before the Lord and ask him to put those things in order. What do you *really* fight for? Let this verse penetrate your heart and mind…

A voice was saying, "Cry out!"
Another said, "What should I cry out?"
"All humanity is grass, and all its goodness is like the flower of the field.

✡ *Isaiah 40:6*

The idea here is that nothing made by human hands lasts forever. There is no man-made monument or institution which is eternal. Only God lives forever, and our greatest achievements are temporary, like wildflowers. So if you store your treasures in heaven, they will never rust.

If you give Yeshua your life, your actions, your mind and heart, he will sustain you beyond the grave, and the battles you fight today will be united with his own.

__OCTOBER. 7__

Many people mistakenly think God is distant, aloof, and even cruel. After all, they reason, why would he allow so many terrible things to take place? But the truth is, he is walking with us every step of the way, even carrying us forward, and sharing in our journey as we forge ahead. Have you ever considered that God has genuine interest in what you do? Ponder this…

He protects his flock like a shepherd;
he gathers the lambs in his arms
and carries them in the fold of his garment.
He gently leads those that are nursing.

✡ *Isaiah 40:11*

You may not understand the difficult and painful situation you are going through, but someday the Lord, the good Shepherd, who acts as your protector, will reveal to you the reasons for your earthly struggles. When that day comes, you will understand that his heart was invested in you every step of the way.

Pray today for other people, other sheep who need his help too. "Loving Lord, a dear friend of mine is trying to make it…"

<u>OCTOBER. 8</u>

The power of our God is supernatural, never ending, and holy. To worship him is the only right human response. No other being in the universe is worthy of our complete love and devotion. But as finite creatures, we can only love God with our limited strength. Fortunately, he is able to cause us – *sinners!* – to worship him in spirit and in truth.

Who has measured the waters in the hollow of his hand
or marked off the heavens with the span of his hand?
Who has gathered the dust of the earth in a measure
or weighed the mountains on a balance
and the hills on the scales?

✡ *Isaiah 40:12*

There is no royalty, no earthly king, who merits what God rightly deserves. Read today's verse again, and consider the poetic wording. How much dirt can you carry in a single bucket? God's hand is large enough to contain the entirety of the Earth.

Worship him with all your heart today, in whatever way he leads you. If you are not sure how to proceed, you might pray along these lines: "Dear God, please teach me what it means to worship you. Please guide me into a life of worship…"

OCTOBER. 9

Imagine what it might be like to hear the actual voice of God. Would it be a thrill? Would it be a shattering catastrophe? Perhaps it would be both. Either way, your Bible is the best source for you to *hear directly* from the Lord. But only in certain places does the Scripture quote God as specifically talking about himself in the first person. Today's verse is just such a case. Consider the questions God poses here to all mankind, including you and I...

"To whom will you compare me, or who is my equal?" asks the Holy One

✡ *Isaiah 40:25*

Truth be told, we worship a God who is unlike anyone or anything else in all of reality. No one is his equal, and nobody measures up to him – not even by a long shot. So when he asks the questions above, he intends for us to consider our perspectives. *"To whom will you compare me? Or who is my equal?"*

Has something or someone become a little god in your life? If so, put things in the right order. Take care to live your days out by worshipping the only true God! You will not ever regret humbling yourself before the Holy One of Israel. His grace and strength are enough to bring you from death into life.

<u>OCTOBER. 10</u>

The faithwalk is one of great hopes, and sometimes great fears. If you have ever wondered how to practice obeying God, one of the best examples you can follow is that of the patriarch Abraham. Allow the example of his ancient faithwalk to influence the way you walk with Yeshua today. In time, you may find that you have something in common with that great man of faith.

By faith Abraham, when he was called, obeyed and set out for a place that he was going to receive as an inheritance. He went out, even though he did not know where he was going.

✡ *Hebrews 11:8*

Stepping out in faith requires trusting God to direct you to your final destination. It requires obedience. Pray about your plans, giving them all over to Yeshua. When you do so, allow the Lord to make any changes he desires along the way. If things end up different than you expected, you can thank God for divinely guiding you to where he wanted you to go.

Today, begin prayer like so: "Loving Lord, even though I cannot see the future, I trust you to show me where to take my next steps…"

OCTOBER. 11

In your travels you will sometimes be confronted by strange people, and places which do not feel like home to you. That is how every child of God feels from time to time – out of place in the world. But sometimes it is best not to become so comfortable here. In your own faithwalk, like Abraham, be prepared to wait for God even when this life feels utterly foreign to you.

By faith he stayed as a foreigner in the land of promise, living in tents as did Isaac and Jacob, coheirs of the same promise.

✡ *Hebrews 11:9*

Eventually this old world will be made entirely new, and so will you. At this moment you live in a temporary tent, which is your body, an imperfect and easily breakable frame. In truth, you are a traveler, passing through this strange land, waiting on God to finally drive away all the evils of this world. And one day you will live in a new mansion of a body, in a re-created universe, to the praise of Yeshua the Messiah. Go to him in prayer today.

<u>OCTOBER. 12</u>

The sustaining hope which comes from the crosswork of Yeshua is our source of joy and freedom. Because he loved us, because he cared for us, and because he desired our own personal restoration, he submitted to the most terrible death. But he knew what was on the other side, and we can look forward to the same goal his eyes were fixed on. Now consider how Abraham viewed his own road of faith, as it stretched out before him…

For he was looking forward to the city that has foundations, whose architect and builder is God.

✡ *Hebrews 11:10*

There is a place, a city, some actual realm in which God is laying down the foundation for an exciting eternity. Yeshua is the cornerstone of the building, and our lives are built upon him.

When times are rough, and you feel small and weak, allow him to be strong for you, and lift your eyes to the heavens. Your future is secure, and there is a great reason for such high hopes: *The Lord is with you!* Take time to invite him into your heart once again.

OCTOBER. 13

The gift you will receive from God, through Yeshua, is beyond description. All your lost hopes and dreams, along with ideas which you have had to set aside, or regrets which plague you with sadness – all of these will be beautifully resolved. He will clear away everything that has ever held you down, and give you wings in exchange.

By faith even Sarah herself, when she was unable to have children, received power to conceive offspring, even though she was past the age, since she considered that the one who had promised was faithful.

✡ *Hebrews 11:11*

Every sin will be summarily washed away. Every mother who longed to hold her baby but couldn't, will be able to do so. Every broken heart and relationship will be mended and perfectly restored. And every shattered person will leap for joy. All of this is because God, the maker and king of our faith, is true to his word.

Maybe you should sing a song of praise today. Or perhaps you should breathe deeply in silence. Allow God to lead you. As you ponder his glory, what is he putting on your heart?

<u>OCTOBER. 14</u>

There is no telling what God will do with your life. It may seem less than glorious to you, living and dying. But your personal touch and ministry to others around you will most certainly have ripple effects. Your life has enormous significance, even if people tell you otherwise. God does not have the limited vision people have; he can do astonishing things with an ordinary person. Again, consider Abraham, your father in the faith…

Therefore, from one man — in fact, from one as good as dead — came offspring as numerous as the stars of the sky and as innumerable as the grains of sand along the seashore.

✡ *Hebrews 11:12*

We consider things in terms of numbers, dollar signs, points, stats, and concrete measurements. But God holds all things in the palm of his hand. Yeshua pointed to the birds, and the flowers. Was any earthly king so well cared-for as they are? The next time you have a chance, step outside and consider these ordinary miracles: The sky, the stars, birds, trees…

When you look at life through the lens of God's eternal love, nothing can shake you. Let *him* be your comfort and security. His plans for you far outstrip the most imaginative human dreamer.

OCTOBER. 15

God desires all the glory for the great things he has done. And rightfully so! It is tempting for us as people to think God has a huge ego, and wants to be praised for the same reasons human beings seek praise. As fallen creatures, we want praise for all the wrong reasons, but there is none like God, who is only good, and purely righteous.

Who has measured the waters in the hollow of his hand or marked off the heavens with the span of his hand? Who has gathered the dust of the earth in a measure or weighed the mountains on a balance and the hills on the scales?

✡ *Isaiah 40:12*

The answer to these questions is meant to be obvious: No one but God alone. The Lord of the universe has measured the oceans, and mountains are not timeless to him, as they seem to us. We pass through this world like a sunset, but he is ancient beyond time and space. Nothing in all creation predates him, and nothing will outlast him.

In light of all this, isn't the promise of eternal life all the more wondrous? That is his plan for you, in Yeshua. You will not melt away like snow, because he will raise you from the dead with a body meant for kingdom life, which never ends. Isn't that a great reason why he does, in fact, deserve *all the glory*, for all the right reasons?

You might just praise him for this today!

OCTOBER. 16

When we try to squeeze God into our own tiny understanding, we do ourselves harm. God is not a subject to be studied in a laboratory, he is the rightful focus of all human worship. As such, our faith in him must allow for categories and realities which do not conform to our limited imaginations. The Lord himself asks the following questions in Isaiah, which are meant to get us thinking…

This is what the Lord says: Heaven is my throne, and earth is my footstool. Where could you possibly build a house for me? And where would my resting place be?

✡ *Isaiah 66:1*

Obviously we will not be building a house for God, he is building us into a holy city! When we understand ourselves as his children, then we have a proper perspective. God is in the process of rescuing us from sin and death; we are entirely unable to do this for ourselves.

In prayer today, surrender everything to him. He takes pleasure in his relationship with you, and wants to hear your prayers and concerns. Maybe start with, "Dear Lord, please govern and guide my life…"

OCTOBER. 17

Materialism is something of a religion in our day. People absolutely love their *things*. But ordinary things can become idols when we cannot see ourselves living apart from them. The best defense against this type of sin is to hold everything God gives you with open hands. He has blessed you with the gifts of life, food, shelter, relationships, and final salvation – all of which come from his hand.

My hand made all these things, and so they all came into being.

✡ *Isaiah 66:2*

The Lord owns the universe. He is the ruler of all, and there is not a rock or tree which he did not create. In a very real sense, even the clothes on your back are on loan. But most importantly, he wants your heart. He has given you volition, the freedom to decide, and you can choose to walk with him, if you are wise. The wonderful twist is, when you give him all that you are, he gives you *all* things.

OCTOBER. 18

In keeping with the theme of giving everything to God, starting with your heart and soul, we are given some great help from the Scriptures. The Lord has a perspective which goes far beyond the surface, and the material. He does not judge you based on your looks or your wealth! Instead, he looks at the heart.

I will look favorably on this kind of person: one who is humble, submissive in spirit, and trembles at my word.

✡ *Isaiah 66:2*

Trembling before God means both fear, and excitement. God is very interested in your spiritual posture. Are you arrogant at times? Proud, or boastful? The cure for that is repentance before Yeshua.

Admit your sin to him, and let him cleanse your conscience. All of heaven rejoices when sinners like us come to the Lord!

OCTOBER. 19

In the end, no matter what happens to you, the Lord will pull off a great miracle. It will be something nobody could have dreamt or imagined. The creativity of God is boundless, and his ability to surprise and overjoy his people is glorious. Today, after you have really given yourself time to quiet your heart before him, ponder the meaning of this stunning verse.

Before Zion was in labor, she gave birth; before she was in pain, she delivered a boy.

✡ *Isaiah 66:7*

Does this verse make sense to you? It is very different from human experience. Can you imagine childbirth without labor pains? Read it again.

In this passage, the woman is actually Jerusalem. She will have a son, it says, and as we will see, many other children soon follow. They are the children of God, and as such, they reflect the deep love God has for his holy city, which are comprised of his *people*.

Allow this amazing truth to grow in your thoughts today. Children born without pain? How can that be? Yet how wonderful it is to be his child!

<u>OCTOBER. 20</u>

Again we return to the idea of children born without pain, in a single moment. With this imagery, the prophet Isaiah gives us a glimpse of what the New Jerusalem will be like, as she who once was barren welcomes her children home.

Who has heard of such a thing? Who has seen such things? Can a land be born in one day or a nation be delivered in an instant? Yet as soon as Zion was in labor, she gave birth to her sons.

✡ *Isaiah 66:8*

One thing the Lord loves to do is turn despair into ecstatic joy. Just when things seem completely hopeless and impossible, he transforms everything, and makes the dead come to life. He does not neglect the childless, or the barren, or the downtrodden.

This life may have its thorns, but his promises remain true. In your prayer time today, make room for something new; make room for the unexpected!

OCTOBER. 21

There is such thing as a *godly patriotism*, detached from earthly politics, but filled with heavenly hope. Only God can make permanent, irreversible, righteous change come about in this fallen world. No social program could ever do what the King of Kings has planned for his creation. He is re-making the universe, and nothing will ever be the same. Even the old city of Jerusalem will become new.

Be glad for Jerusalem and rejoice over her, all who love her. Rejoice greatly with her, all who mourn over her.

✡ *Isaiah 66:10*

This verse connects to the imagery of childbirth without pain. When God brings his people home, to the New Jerusalem, there will be a celebration, the likes of which humanity has never seen. So the word is out on the street! Spread the word!

What can you do in your own days to anticipate the coming Kingdom of Messiah? Step out in faith! And always pray for wisdom. "Dear Lord, please show me how to live in expectation…"

<u>OCTOBER. 22</u>

Self-discovery is a natural part of curiosity about our identity as people. Have you ever wondered, "Who am I?" That is the central question concerning *identity*. But in this sad age, many people are overly obsessed with their personal identity, to the point where they are unable to look outside themselves for life's answers. If self-focus has plagued you to some degree, it is time to look to The One who made you; it is time to look to the Lord.

I — I am the one who comforts you. Who are you that you should fear humans who die, or a son of man who is given up like grass?

✡ *Isaiah 51:12*

When you truly find your identity in Yeshua, you will no longer feel the need to identify yourself with something unhealthy or unwise. However you may have seen yourself before, he will focus and clarify it all for you. You are more than the sum of your fears and insecurities.

Look to him and he will help you, because no mortal man can do what Yeshua has already done on your behalf. Finish this prayer: "Dear God, be my great comfort, I am very concerned with…"

OCTOBER. 23

Through his crosswork, the Lord Yeshua clears a salvation path which is straight and true. He took on a human nature, so as to mediate forgiveness between God and man. Through his sacrifice, those of us who want to be free from the prisons of sin and death can run to God for our liberation. Pray over this verse today, and allow it to sink in deep.

The prisoner is soon to be set free; he will not die and go to the Pit, and his food will not be lacking.

✡ *Isaiah 51:14*

The Lord will not neglect you. You will not die in a dungeon of sin. He knows about the circumstances you face, and promises not to leave his children in bondage to the devil and the world.

Briefly consider some of the things which have had mastery over you throughout your life. Understand that Yeshua has overcome this world, so you will not struggle with these things forever. How might you celebrate that freedom today?

<u>OCTOBER. 24</u>

We serve a merciful God. He is gentle, loving, compassionate, and eager to forgive. But every living soul experiences troubles, difficult times, and some rainfall. And because of our fallen nature, God knows we need constant correction and guidance. If you understand the Lord as being sovereign over your good times as well as the bad, then you can take hope in the fact that it is not his will for you to suffer endlessly.

Look, I have removed from your hand the cup that causes staggering; that goblet, the cup of my fury. You will never drink it again.

✡ *Isaiah 51:22*

When God corrects his children it may seem like punishment, but he does not hate his own. Because of Yeshua, we are viewed in a different way than before we came to faith. Whereas you formerly were seen as a sinner, enslaved to your own sin, God now sees you through the crosswork of his son, Yeshua, who is the forerunner of our faith, blazing a trail into heaven. Follow him with all your might! God will not make you stagger in your race, and someday every sorrow you have ever had will turn into joy.

In prayer, allow him to take the 'cup that made you stagger' out of your hand today.

OCTOBER. 25

There is enormous soul power in the faithwalk with Yeshua. No other being in the universe holds the ability to command the oceans, shake the earth, and raise the dead. Since he has risen, the will of God is executed through the Holy Spirit, in the heart of every believer. Think about that – God himself is active *inside of you.* There may be times when you feel far from him, but he is ever present, and working in your life from the inside out. And what is most beautiful, is that he will never give notice and vacate!

I baptize you with water for repentance, but the one who is coming after me is more powerful than I. I am not worthy to remove his sandals. He himself will baptize you with the Holy Spirit and fire.

✡ *Matthew 3:11*

When you gave your life to Yeshua, he entered your heart, and effectively put to death your old sin nature, along with your former hell-bound destiny. It will die a slow death, giving you problems as long as you live, but you are a new creature in him. And as such, your inclinations, your tastes, your sensibilities, your destiny – everything about you – is now oriented toward God in holiness. He has baptized you with the Holy Spirit and fire.

OCTOBER. 26

Begin your devotional time with praise to God. If you are tired, it does not need to be with dancing and singing. You need only tell him how you love him. Thank the Lord for his goodness toward you, and allow him to break your impulse to hold onto stresses and worries. Sometimes a new perspective is needed, and you can best hear from God in prayer when you have surrendered it all to him.

When Jesus was baptized, he went up immediately from the water. The heavens suddenly opened for him, and he saw the Spirit of God descending like a dove and coming down on him.

✡ *Matthew 3:16*

Have you ever wondered why Yeshua was baptized? He was not a sinner. It is thought by scholars that he submitted to baptism in order to immerse himself fully in the human experience, and to coronate a new ministry. You need not be re-baptized if you are starting something brand new, but if you have undergone a major change, it is perfectly acceptable to do so. In any case, rest today knowing that your Lord and Savior has done it all, and your experiences – as strange as some of them may be – are not at all foreign to him.

OCTOBER. 27

You may see yourself in all sorts of negative ways. Deep inside you might even see yourself as worthless and insignificant. But Yeshua sees you as his friend. He is on your side, 'til the end, every step of the way. He sees you as priceless, precious, beautiful, talented, and worth loving. Turn your thoughts toward him, and consider this amazing passage...

And a voice from heaven said: "This is my beloved Son, with whom I am well-pleased."

✡ *Matthew 3:17*

As a follower of Yeshua you are not simply a fan, or an autograph seeker. He knows you too well for that, and he has time for you personally. He is pleased with you and protective of you, as you walk along with him, trusting God to carry you home.

When you finally meet him face-to-face, he will commend you and reward you in front of both angels and men. On that day, his tremendous blessing of recognition will never be taken from you, and you will never see yourself in a poor light again. For now, turn to him in personal prayer.

<u>OCTOBER. 28</u>

Your God is looking out for you. Before you wake up in the morning, he already has your day planned. You may have walked with Yeshua for most of your life, or you may be a new believer, but the truth is still the same: The God of all creation takes pride in you, and sees you as someone worth dying for. Because of his painful and humiliating sacrifice on the cross, you will be spared from the consequences of your own sin nature. He will lift your head up to the heavens, and give you a new identity in him.

Do not be afraid, for you will not be put to shame; don't be humiliated, for you will not be disgraced.

✡ *Isaiah 54:4*

The Lord is in the process of re-making you from the inside out. God is devoted to your well-being, to the point that he has taken the full punishment of sin on your behalf, giving you the freedom to come home. He has done all this to show you how great his love is.

Today, take time to let Yeshua shape your view of these things. He is trustworthy, so trust him! Complete this prayer: "Loving Lord, today I trust you with…"

OCTOBER. 29

In every relationship there is tension. The best couples struggle with understanding each another, and the same goes for parents and children. We are called by Yeshua to approach the Lord with the same demeanor as that of a child – unassuming, trusting, and in need. But children often need to be protected from themselves, and kept from doing things which are harmful. And without thinking, we can anger God by sinning carelessly.

In a surge of anger I hid my face from you for a moment, but I will have compassion on you with everlasting love," says the Lord your Redeemer.

✡ *Isaiah 54:8*

If it seems difficult to understand God as being angry, stop and think about whose image you were created in. You have a full range of emotions, and so does the Lord. But when he becomes angry, it is a righteous anger which does not sin. Most often, when he is angry, it is a *protective* anger which is looking out for innocent people.

Pray today that your relationship with him would grow, and that those things which anger him would also anger you. Moreover, pray that your love and compassion would mirror his as well.

<u>OCTOBER. 30</u>

When the earth was first made, God formed it out of chaos and disorder. He spoke order, light, and life into the world. Such is the wisdom of God! But someday the end will come. And even though people like to imagine life as being like a wheel, going round and round, the truth is that history has a beginning, a middle, and an end. Time is linear, not cyclical, and the story is moving forward. So when the end of all things comes, creation will once again turn back to chaos and disorder, before finally being transformed and renewed.

Though the mountains move and the hills shake, my love will not be removed from you and my covenant of peace will not be shaken," says your compassionate Lord.

✡ *Isaiah 54:10*

This verse gives us great hope. Even when the world falls apart, the love of God will not fail. His promises will remain forever, even beyond space and time. Entire mountains may crumble into the sea, but Yeshua has secured your future by his everlasting love. In your prayer time today, let the Lord work in your heart, and guide the story of your life.

OCTOBER. 31

If you have ever struggled with money, or resources, there is something beautiful you should know. Your loving heavenly Father has riches beyond imagination, so your hope should rest in him. In the Bible we read of streets paved with gold, which may seem quaint to our modern sensibilities. But the idea is that there will be no lack, anywhere, for anyone in the Kingdom of God. He will more than provide for all your needs.

Come, everyone who is thirsty, come to the water;
and you without silver, come, buy, and eat!
Come, buy wine and milk without silver and without cost!

✡ *Isaiah 55:1*

The offer of salvation is a free one. You do not need to prove yourself, or fill out an application. You need only receive Yeshua into your heart by faith. He knows you struggle, and he knows about your hurts. That's why he says, "Come!" He has invited you to a free meal, a banquet which never ends, and you have a place at the table with the King. He has paid for your ticket, and your transportation will be on the wings of angels.

__NOVEMBER 1__

Take time to tune it all out. Turn off the noise, put aside the gadgets, and feel the quiet. Let your heart be still. Your God is alive and real, wanting to reach through, and penetrate your heart. Your loving heavenly Father is also your best friend in the universe. Through Yeshua, the Son of God, you have become a part of the royal family of the Kingdom of Heaven. Your place is in the throne room of Messiah, and he is calling you there.

Listen carefully to me, and eat what is good, and you will enjoy the choicest of foods.

✡ *Isaiah 55:2*

No talk show host, no pop star, no politician or infamous personality has the power to offer you what God is giving you freely through Yeshua. Because of this, he is insistent that you listen! God does not speak in order to be ignored.

For our own good he reminds us to do the right thing, sort of like eating our vegetables. But the great banquet he has invited you to will be a lavish affair, and will nourish your very soul.

In prayer today, savor your time with the God of the universe. You might continue your devotional time by reading the verse again, and then sitting in silence, listening.

NOVEMBER 2

Today, as you consider what lies ahead of you, remember to replenish your soul with prayers and thanksgiving. Not only is the Lord with you, but there is a great multitude of others who are part of his family as well. As a member of the covenant people, you are afforded great privileges.

Pay attention and come to me; listen, so that you will live.
I will make a permanent covenant with you on the basis of the faithful kindnesses of David.

✡*Isaiah 55:3*

There is no greater gift than the love of God, and he gives it generously. He loved King David, and promised to expand his kingdom into something eternal. Through the Savior, Yeshua, that earthly kingdom has become transcendent and supernatural. So when you prepare for the Messiah, you are preparing for something much bigger than ordinary routine; you are being prepared for eternity.

Walk humbly, live quietly, and share the blessed truth you have been given with others. If you are alert, you may even be able to help change a life.

NOVEMBER 3

The story of the Bible is God's story, and you are a part of it through Yeshua. He has an expansive plotline, with a great finale in store at the end. As a believer and follower of the Messiah, you are part of a huge cast of real life characters, involved in the drama of the heavens. Jerusalem is the central location of the story, and when God looks at the holy city, he sees a past filled with idolatry and spiritual adultery. But when he returns, that city will be flooded with God's people, all streaming in, to rejoice and give glory to the Lord.

Raise your eyes and look around: they all gather and come to you; your sons will come from far away, and your daughters on the hips of nannies.

✡ *Isaiah 60:4*

God speaks of Jerusalem as if she is a surprised mother, welcoming her children home for the most amazing family reunion. She has been deserted and war torn, but that will not always be the case.

As you consider your own place in God's larger story, pray for sensitivity to spiritual matters. It is not always easy to navigate the faithwalk, but you are one of his children, and a great family gathering is on your own horizon.

<u>NOVEMBER 4</u>

Focusing your thoughts on God once again, your future is indeed bright, even if today is dark and difficult. Your place in the Kingdom is secure, thanks to Yeshua. You have been redeemed through his crosswork! In your devotional time today, consider once again the promise God has made to those who follow him, and the excitement which will rush through the re-constituted Jerusalem one bright day.

Then you will see and be radiant, and your heart will tremble and rejoice, because the riches of the sea will become yours and the wealth of the nations will come to you.

✡ *Isaiah 60:5*

When Yeshua returns for his people, there will be no poverty of any sort. All the riches of God will be poured out, so that nobody will be left wanting. And the entire raging world will become subservient when The King returns.

In your quiet time today, ask the Lord to give you his peace, and to shape your faith, so that you might be ready when The Day comes, when your heart too will swell with joy. You might begin your prayers with, "Loving Lord, I praise you, and accept your invitation…"

<u>NOVEMBER 5</u>

In the quiet of your heart, take a few moments to be still before the Lord. You are safe when you come before God, and he is always ready to meet you in prayer. Although this world is ugly and dark, God is working his plan of redemption. Despite the hardships you face, it will all be worth it in the end. When you are at ease, give some thought to this imagery from Isaiah...

Your city gates will always be open; they will never be shut day or night so that the wealth of the nations may be brought into you, with their kings being led in procession.

✡ *Isaiah 60:11*

In our daily routines it is easy sometimes to lose sight of the end goal, but the final destiny of your life is in the eternal Kingdom of Yeshua. Everything will be resplendent in the glory of God, in a grand parade, and the universe itself will be set right.

If you feel small today, or weak, ask him to fill your heart once again. You can never scrape the bottom of God's resources in prayer. Pray for forgiveness, peace, and strength in our Lord.

NOVEMBER 6

Waiting is a spiritual discipline. We give our tithes, abstain from sin, pray regularly, and attend worship services. But all of these things are a part of waiting on the Lord's return. In your walk with Yeshua you will find many diversions and distractions, things to fill your time. But pairing your activities with an expectant heart is the key to active waiting. Also, one of the most important aspects of the faithwalk is Scripture study, and verses like the following can enrich your soul when you review them throughout your day.

Violence will never again be heard of in your land; devastation and destruction will be gone from your borders. You will call your walls Salvation and your city gates Praise.

✡ *Isaiah 60:18*

The city of God will be filled with his peace, and his people will constitute that city. We can barely imagine what the New Jerusalem will be like in actuality, but we can fully expect that the bride of Yeshua will be a holy population, dedicated to his praise and honor. The famous expression, "a land without a people for a people without a land," will take on a whole new meaning when God's people enter his Kingdom.

In prayer today, meditate on his great mercy, yet be still inside, as you continue to practice waiting on him.

NOVEMBER 7

Make no mistake, God is alive and well, and on the move. It may seem at times like he has forgotten the world, and left us for naught, but nothing could be further from the truth. The Lord is almighty, and seated on the throne of authority and power. He can, and will, take the smallest, most humble of all people, and cause unimaginable growth. If we could see today what he will ultimately do with the most meager of us, we would be staggered.

The least will become a thousand, the smallest a mighty nation. I am the Lord; I will accomplish it quickly in its time.

✡ *Isaiah 60:22*

In the repetitive groove of daily life, it may not occur to you just how quickly the Lord's Day will arrive. Too many people have been lulled into a false sense of security, thinking that God is not watching, is unaware, and not at all concerned – if he even exists! But nobody keeps his word like the Lord, our God. At just the right time, he will bring forth an entirely new nation and creation, all with breathtaking speed.

Ask your Heavenly Father to remember you, and to give you a sense of his presence today as you pray.

NOVEMBER 8

The ascension of Yeshua into the heavens is one of the most misunderstood doctrines. We read that he went up into the clouds, and our impression is that he simply floated into outer space! But the *cloud* which enveloped him was likely the quality of cloud which the Bible uses to describe the Presence of God. We see it during the wanderings in the wilderness of Sinai, and at the Transfiguration. This is the glory cloud of God's temple.

And while he was blessing them, he left them and was carried up into heaven.

✡ *Luke 24:51*

By virtue of his ascension, Yeshua has opened heaven up to ordinary people. His resurrection made clear that death is not the invincible force. Since death is a defeated foe, and heaven is a thrilling destiny for the people of God, Yeshua is to be praised to the ends of the earth, all our earthly lives.

As you prepare now for the days ahead, consider the great and eternal Sabbath rest which awaits you in heaven.

<u>NOVEMBER 9</u>

In our modern world it is so easy to lose heart, become bitter, walk away from the Lord, and lose all hope. There is no shortage of pain and suffering in our day, and our own needs are thrown in along with everyone else's. What do to? How do we trust God when we don't see Him? Settle your heart, and pray over this verse…

Therefore, as the Holy Spirit says: Today, if you hear his voice, do not harden your hearts as in the rebellion, on the day of testing in the wilderness, where your fathers tested me, tried me, and saw my works.

✡ *Hebrews 3:7-9*

The ancient Hebrews walked through hot sandy deserts, struggling with their faith. Many lost heart, and did not make it into the Promised Land. We are encouraged to walk a different path. If you can cling to God, even though you may have lost all strength, he will restore you, refresh you, and bring you into his presence. Do not give up on God!

Complete this prayer: "Dear Lord, strengthen my heart, and help me trust you for…"

NOVEMBER 10

In the stillness of your devotional time, carefully consider your own state of mind. Are you ready to be receptive to what the Lord has for you today? Maybe you need to remain still for a while longer, and do some business with God. He is always there to help soften your spirit, to give you peace, and allow you to be cleansed of all sin, through Yeshua.

Watch out, brothers and sisters, so that there won't be in any of you an evil, unbelieving heart that turns away from the living God.

✡ *Hebrews 3:12*

It is the subject of great debate, whether we turn to God, or God calls us. Perhaps it is both, as two people – you and Yeshua – enter into a relationship. So he has given you a new heart, and your job is to give it back to him.

Is there something you've been holding back from God? Are there doubts inside, which prevent you from walking in true freedom? If so, never fear. God wants to walk with you through those doubts, enabling you to trust in him more, the older you get, the wiser you become.

NOVEMBER 11

If you have a handful of close friends, who stand by you through thick and thin, you are blessed. Your best friends will tell you hard truths, and push you to keep going, even when you feel like giving up. One way to cultivate spiritual strength, is to practice encouragement with your friends, as this verse instructs…

But encourage each other daily, while it is still called today, so that none of you is hardened by sin's deception.

✡ *Hebrews 3:13*

Nobody is meant to walk the path of faith all alone. God has called a vast community of believers out of this world, binding them together through the blood of Yeshua, so that we might all help one another to navigate our way home to the Lord. But in this life, there are only so many steps along the way, only so many "todays" to experience! Be sure to make the most of each day, doing what you can to help other believers avoid the pitfalls of sin, and to prayerfully walk with Yeshua yourself.

Today – *along with thanking a veteran!* – you might pray along these lines: "Dear Heavenly Father, while it is today, I really need help with…"

NOVEMBER 12

As the season moves along, be sure to slow down and consult with God. Do you need to make a course correction? Maybe you've made some missteps recently. If so, now is a perfect time to start afresh. God knows how best to guide you, so rest in his promises. Sometimes going back to basics is the most important thing we can do.

For we have become participants in Christ if we hold firmly until the end the reality that we had at the start.

✡ *Hebrews 3:14*

It is an historical truth, a fact, that Yeshua has risen from the dead. Many witnesses attested to this reality. Even still, for those of us who await his return, it is often difficult to connect with God when we, ourselves, have become so 'sophisticated.'

Return to the cross today, in your mind's eye. Remember what originally broke your heart. Become child-like again, and give God the brokenness of your life. In prayer today, ask him to deepen your roots, and strengthen your faith. He is making all things new, including you.

<u>NOVEMBER 13</u>

Your Heavenly Father never tires. He never sleeps, never wearies, and does not run out of energy to get the job done. Because of this, you can take heart – he will not forget his promises, and he won't neglect you. The Lord will complete his work of salvation and renewal in your life, just like he finished his original work of creation…

Therefore, a Sabbath rest remains for God's people. For the person who has entered his rest has rested from his own works, just as God did from his.

✡ *Hebrews 4:9-10*

One day all your pain and worries will be gone, and you will find rest. But this is not the sort of rest that comes from pure exhaustion. The Sabbath rest of God is one that invigorates, re-charges, and brings to life everything that ever died. The Sabbath rest of Yeshua will be a thrill and a joy. That is what we look forward to.

Ask God to give you vision and hope today. Pray, "Dear God, I often become very tired, but I trust you to…"

<u>NOVEMBER 14</u>

As your days unfold, have a sober mind. Do not rush out and do foolish things, but take stock instead. This is the time to connect with God again. Did you set some things right recently? What has the Lord put on your plate for today and tomorrow? Whatever may have transpired, now is the time to prepare your whole self for worshipping him.

Let us then make every effort to enter that rest, so that no one will fall into the same pattern of disobedience.

✡ *Hebrews 4:11*

Each day you walk with the Lord brings you a little closer to the marvelous destiny he has planned for you. The road you walk may be full of sorrow and pain, but do not become bitter or hard hearted. Let the Lord refresh you again, and give you the resolve that you will never truly rest until you reach the Kingdom of Heaven. In Yeshua there is life, and he is your ultimate destination.

As God works in your heart over time, allow his ideas and thoughts to come alive inside you. If you love this world more than you love him, you will be lost. So today, exert your spiritual muscles, and do whatever he calls you to do, so that your life will become a testimony to his mercy and grace.

<u>NOVEMBER 15</u>

Man wishes to see himself as larger than he really is. Psalm 8 teaches us that we are actually a little below the angels, but one significant step above the animals. We are *creaturely*, but the angels are our peers. And yet, in the vastness of all creation, we forget how temporary we really are, and how small we are – like grass, or melting snow. Consider the way in which God looks down on the earth.

Do you not know? Have you not heard? Has it not been declared to you from the beginning? Have you not considered the foundations of the earth?
God is enthroned above the circle of the earth; its inhabitants are like grasshoppers. He stretches out the heavens like thin cloth and spreads them out like a tent to live in.

✡ *Isaiah 40:21-22*

This passage gives us a surprising indication that, yes, we *do* know, and yes, we *have* heard, from the beginning, all about God. People want to pretend that man invented God, without proof of his existence, but this passage indicts us all. God will not let mankind feign ignorance.

In light of his higher point of view – the God's eye view – it is deeply comforting to know he is also looking out for the little people, we, his children.

NOVEMBER 16

Turning again to God for guidance and help, make sure you are in a comfortable place, with a quiet heart, and an eager mind. Your thoughts may be scattered, but if you slow things down, and ask the Holy Spirit for his peace, you will find that God's presence is never far. Take time again to consider the picture of childbirth, as it relates to Jerusalem at the end of time…

Who has heard of such a thing? Who has seen such things? Can a land be born in one day or a nation be delivered in an instant? Yet as soon as Zion was in labor, she gave birth to her sons.

✡ *Isaiah 66:8*

If the New Jerusalem is to be the city of God, then it will most certainly have its inhabitants. And where will they come from? They will be children of the living God! Yet somehow, despite all the warfare that ancient city has seen over the ages, there will at once be a new nation birthed from the ashes of human history. All without labor pains!

That is the miracle Isaiah is describing for us. Can you imagine yourself as part of such an amazing work? Allow God to deepen your perspective on who you are in him.

<u>NOVEMBER 17</u>

Believe it or not, God commands his people to rejoice. You may not feel like it, but there is much more to rejoicing than dancing around and singing praises. Rejoicing in the Lord calls for a deep internal connection with the truth of what he has done for you. When you know God is in your corner, there is nothing that can shake your shalom. Consider this…

Be glad for Jerusalem and rejoice over her, all who love her. Rejoice greatly with her, all who mourn over her.

✡ *Isaiah 66:10*

If Jerusalem is like barren woman who has longed for children, then our love for her prompts us to rejoice when she becomes a mother with *countless* children. As one of God's children yourself, can you find reasons to rejoice in the future plans of God? The hope and destiny of every believer is wrapped up in the blessing of God's Jerusalem.

<u>NOVEMBER 18</u>

God's loves Jerusalem like a good husband loves his bride. A husband cannot be a true husband without dearly loving his beloved! And when a man loves his wife he gives her everything in his ability. After all, she is worth more than gold and precious gems! With that in mind, take time to recall the things of the year so far, and let the Lord soothe your worried mind. You are a child of the King! One day you will reside in his household...

I will make peace flow to her like a river, and the wealth of nations like a flood; you will nurse and be carried on her hip and bounced on her lap.

✡ *Isaiah 66:12*

In this verse God is pouring on Jerusalem every opulence and luxury imaginable, along with his wonderful shalom. And did you notice Jerusalem nursing her children? Carrying them around, and bouncing them on her knee? That's you in there! You are one of God's kids, and he sees you as a child and resident of the holy city, playing affectionately like a mother with her baby.

If you have ever doubted that God loves you, put that notion aside. He sees you as a baby, in need. And if you cry out to him today, he will certainly meet you, even in your adult problems and worries.

<u>NOVEMBER 19</u>

It is important to recognize God as he wants to be understood. Yeshua referred to the Lord as his Father – Abba. In light of this, it is wise to respect the Lord's wishes, and to look up to him as a Heavenly Father. Sometimes that can be difficult, especially for those who have had bad experiences, or no experiences, with human fathers. If that is you, consider the following…

As a mother comforts her son, so I will comfort you, and you will be comforted in Jerusalem.

✡ *Isaiah 66:13*

The Lord is capable of immense emotion toward his people. Your earthly mother and father may have been less than they ought to have been, but God sees you with a heart full of fondness and tenderness. He is the ultimate parent! Even the strongest men in the world are reduced to tears in light of God's love and healing grace.

If you need to receive the comfort of your Heavenly Father, don't wait. Cry out to him today.

NOVEMBER 20

God's promises will be stunning to see come to fruition. There is a plan, a hope, and a direction to human history. We have not been abandoned. Take some time today to look back on the seasons, and reflect on your prayers. Also remember the New Jerusalem – a barren woman who yearns to have babies, and who will be miraculously blessed with a multitude of children, and without birth pains! You are one of those children, and these promises will directly affect you.

You will see, you will rejoice, and you will flourish like grass; then the Lord's power will be revealed to his servants, but he will show his wrath against his enemies.

✡ *Isaiah 66:14*

The Day of the Lord is coming, and it will be fearful and wonderful. Ask the Lord to prepare you for what he has in the future. He will judge the world, and set everything straight. Sin will be gone, and death will be a thing of the past. Pray today for wisdom and a strong heart. You will need the help of your Heavenly Father to get where you are going today.

<u>NOVEMBER 21</u>

Prayer allows you to come into contact with the Creator of the universe. What a great honor! Believe it or not, the Lord of all creation wants to spend time with you. So clear your schedule, settle yourself down, and give him your full attention. The world can wait. Once you have centered your focus on God, and invited him into your heart and mind, ask him to open your eyes, so that you can see the things of eternity breaking into the temporal world.

If I have told you about earthly things and you don't believe, how will you believe if I tell you about heavenly things?

✡ *John 3:12-13*

All around you are solid physical objects which are breaking apart. The same goes for your own body. Over time everything disintegrates, and turns back into dust. But the permanent reality of God's Kingdom is underneath it all, slowly breaking in. As our world dies, his Kingdom grows. Yeshua himself tried to explain this to his generation. If you put your faith in him, even though the Kingdom is invisible, one day you will see it.

NOVEMBER 22

It is amazing to consider the love of God. God's love is not fickle, or weak, or passive. He loves like no other person. He loves the unlovable, he loves those who hate themselves, and he loves those who do not deserve it – that's all of us. And the most wonderful truth you can ever take hold of is God's *grace*. The reality of God's grace lets us see that we, in all our wretchedness, have become the beneficiaries of God's blessings.

For God loved the world in this way: He gave his one and only Son, so that everyone who believes in him will not perish but have eternal life.

✡ *John 3:16*

This verse is so popular that it often gets overlooked, and maybe you read it too fast. If so, go back and place your own name in there. God so loved...*you.* When you are completely honest about your own character, do you really appreciate what he has done for you, a sinner? In the big picture of your life, do you deserve to live forever? The reason you can have that hope, is because of his love for you today. You do not need to do anything to earn his love. In fact, he will not accept payment!

NOVEMBER 23

The name of Yeshua is based on a Hebrew verb meaning "save." His name literally means *one who saves*. When we speak of God saving people, we are really talking about a rescue. God has decided to rescue people from certain destruction, and bring them into safety. Imagine yourself sinking in the sea, lost and far from shore. Yeshua did not come into the world to drown you. He came to lift you up.

For God did not send his Son into the world to condemn the world, but to save the world through him.

✡ *John 3:17*

The Savior of the world, Yeshua, is able to rescue you from sin because he was sinless, much the same way a person on solid ground is in a better position to rescue a drowning man. If he were struggling with sin too, he would not be able to rescue you. But God sent him to pull you out. He suffered a death penalty which you could not have endured, and which would have destroyed you. He is strong enough to save you, even from death.

Praise him today, because he came into the hostile world with the best intentions, and came through for you.

NOVEMBER 24

Allow yourself several moments with the Lord before you say anything. It's important to rest in him, and not always fill the precious time with words. Listening to God is as much a part of prayer as speaking. You have far more going on than you can possibly tend to on your own, so let him be in charge. He created you, he knows you, and his purpose for you is to become more heavenly, like him. You might feel dirty and earth bound, but he hasn't given up on you. Unfortunately, so many refuse to embrace him.

This is the judgment: The light has come into the world, and people loved darkness rather than the light because their deeds were evil.

✡ *John 3:19*

To be a sinner in love with your own sin is a perilous position. Remember, the world is dying all around you, and his Kingdom is slowly breaking in. One day everything will be made new, and you will look around and realize the Kingdom of God has fully conquered the world. In order to detach yourself from the darkness, embrace Yeshua fully.

All too often people think they will miss out if they give their lives to Yeshua. The opposite is true: You will gain more than you can imagine, when you hold onto him for dear life.

NOVEMBER 25

If you have had a challenging time, and this season of your life has been difficult, do not despair. There is One who knows you better than anyone in the world, and he sees you as you were meant to be. He sees you as a finished, perfected, radiant child of God. And even your own insecurities cannot get in the way. You may at times feel concerned about your personal history, your failings. Lay those fears to rest, and consider this verse…

For everyone who does evil hates the light and avoids it, so that his deeds may not be exposed.

✡ *John 3:20*

God knows your deeds, yet doesn't hold them against you. He has placed all of your sin onto Yeshua, who died in your place, and rose again, paving the path for your salvation. You do not need to be afraid that God will ridicule you, or exploit your shortcomings. He is not a cruel God like that. He is the best person in the world to trust, because he loves you, and the truth of who you are – and whom you will become – is fully known to him.

<u>NOVEMBER 26</u>

As the year comes to its last weeks, determine to finish strong for Yeshua. Have you been walking with him a long time? Have you been suffering? Have you been struggling with sins which seem never to go away? Maybe your relationships are strained, and you feel like a failure. Give all of that to him in prayer today. Understand that he sees everything, the whole entire mess. You cannot shock or surprise God. He knows you too well.

But anyone who lives by the truth comes to the light, so that his works may be shown to be accomplished by God.

✡ *John 3:21*

If you bring your problems and struggles to the cross of Yeshua, and lay your life before him, then you have come into agreement with this verse. The truth of God is your guide to forgiveness. He cares about you, and wants the best for you. You may regret your sin, and feel sorrow because of what you have done. If not, then you need to understand – God feels sorrow over your sin too, but through Yeshua you have been cleansed, washed clean.

You are never a failure in God's eyes when you come to him openly, asking for mercy, admitting your need. He is your loving heavenly Father.

NOVEMBER 27

One day the Lord will return. On that day he will set everything straight. He will bring perfect justice to the world, and his perfect mercy will reign throughout creation. This idea, this future, is predicted by all the prophets, including Micah. Take a few minutes to settle your heart and invite the Lord into your devotional time. Let the implications of this verse hit you…

I will remove your horses from you and wreck your chariots.

✡ *Micah 5:10*

This picture of destruction envisages the Lord wiping out all military might which would presume to stand against him. There is no earthly or angelic warrior who can overcome the Lord, and presume to humble him. When The Day of the Lord comes, none of his enemies will prevail. In contrast, The Day of the Lord will bring great relief for his true followers, who have been oppressed by corrupt human powers. Those he will utterly destroy.

In prayer now, ask God to allow your humble day to be buoyed overwhelming realities. As you do ordinary routines, remember that extraordinary events are slowly unfolding even now.

NOVEMBER 28

Slow things down, and take a deep breath. The Lord is your friend, and he knows your fears and pains. You have no greater advocate in the universe than Yeshua, and he willingly died for you, to rescue you from destruction. Once again, give your heart and mind to God, and recall that there is, sometime in the future, a Day on the calendar in which the Lord will destroy all sin and evil.

I will remove sorceries from your hands, and you will not have any more fortune-tellers.

✡ *Micah 5:12*

If you have been sucked into divination, sorcery, or any sort of manipulation of familiar spirits, for the sake of entertainment, or for any other reason, cut yourself free from that deadly trap. It only leads to ruin.

Demonic activity is entirely common in many parts of the world, but is becoming more prevalent in the west. God will destroy all of it. If you have been privy to any sort of spiritual evil, cast yourself at the foot of the cross, in the name of Yeshua. He can deliver you, and protect you!

NOVEMBER 29

Close your eyes, set your mind on Yeshua. Keep them closed as long as you need to in order to clear everything else away. In some sense, it is good that we do not yet know what he looks like, because our simple vision of him would become an idol.

God wants us to look to him with the eyes of faith. Someday we will see him in all his glory, but for now, it is best not to trust our own senses too much. Consider again the destruction God will bring on the great and awesome Day of the Lord…

I will remove your carved images and sacred pillars from you so that you will no longer worship the work of your hands.

✡ *Micah 5:13*

Chances are you have not intentionally forged a physical idol. But what do you gaze upon with longing? What items do you hold near and dear to your heart? Make no mistake, God gives you good things because he loves you, but everything belong to him. Can he trust you to steward, and care for – but not to worship – the people and things around you?

Bring this tricky issue to him in prayer. You might start like this: "Loving Lord, please keep me from bowing down to…"

NOVEMBER 30

The Day of the Lord is surely coming. Nothing can stop him or slow him down. Before you rush off into another busy day, give him the best of yourself. Tell him all your problems, worries, and concerns. Do not be afraid to pray deeply personal prayers. Also, do not be afraid to praise him. He is the Lord Almighty, and all of creation testifies to his greatness – so you are right to give him praise! One Day, his Name will be vindicated before all mankind. On that Day, nobody, *nobody* will escape his judgment.

Listen to the Lord's lawsuit, you mountains and enduring foundations of the earth, because the Lord has a case against his people, and he will argue it against Israel.

✡ *Micah 6:2*

It may be difficult to understand God judging his own people. But the earth is his, and everything in it. Consider this verse again, and note how it reads like a lawyer in court making his case. God has a legitimate complaint against his own. They have been unfaithful, just like the rest of the world. But if you are in Yeshua, if you put your faith in him, then he will judge you based on what his Son has done, rather than what you have done. Isn't that worth telling someone about? Pray today for the opportunity!

<u>DECEMBER 1</u>

One thing God calls us to do, is *remember*. Do you remember what he did for you? Do you recall how lost you were before you knew him? Maybe you've gotten far away from your first love, and it's time to return. Remember what God did for you, and remember what it was like when you were content to be alone with him, just you, your Bible, and the Lord. To remember his loving kindness is part of the key to this section of Micah…

My people, what have I done to you, or how have I wearied you? Testify against me! Indeed, I brought you up from the land of Egypt and redeemed you from that place of slavery. I sent Moses, Aaron, and Miriam ahead of you.

✡ *Micah 6:3-4*

In God's lawsuit against his own people, he calls them to consider what he did for them in the great days of the past. Didn't he rescue them from slavery? Didn't he rescue *you* from sin? How could we ever forget that, and turn our backs on the Lord? Never let it happen! God has done right by us, and it is our responsibility never to forget.

Pray today for a heightened sense of gratitude. "Dear Lord, I am so thankful for all the blessings you have freely given, including…"

__DECEMBER 2__

As you come nearer to year's end, let this next verse form your thoughts about today. It is appropriately etched in stone high upon the ornate religion alcove, of the US Library of Congress. It was specifically selected for display because it was thought by our founding fathers to be a summary of all that true religion should consist of. Let the Lord speak to you through this verse…

Mankind, he has told each of you what is good and what it is the Lord requires of you: to act justly, to love faithfulness, and to walk humbly with your God.

✡ *Micah 6:8*

Along with the previous exhortation to *remember* what God has done for you, it is only appropriate that you should turn and *act* on that kindness. The Lord has made his case! He has rescued you from slavery and sin. So now what? Three things: Act justly, love mercy, and walk humbly with him. That is the full summation of what he requires of you, now that you are a disciple of Yeshua.

He wants you to travel along the road with him, throughout your life, in this walk of faith. Ask him today, and he will help you to do those three things: Act justly, love mercy, and walk humbly with him.

DECEMBER 3

Now and again we all need to take personal inventory, with honest consideration towards simplifying our lives. You can do this in devotional time with an eye towards walking closer with the Lord, and blessing other people. Oftentimes, this also calls for a spiritual house cleaning, and removing things which hinder our relationship with God. Pray over the following verses, in which Yeshua does some serious house cleaning.

In the temple he found people selling oxen, sheep, and doves, and he also found the money changers sitting there. After making a whip out of cords, he drove everyone out of the temple with their sheep and oxen. He also poured out the money changers' coins and overturned the tables.

✡ *John 2:14-15*

The Lord is not like mortal man. He does not tolerate sin, and he doesn't have to. In contrast, all too often we accommodate sin, say nothing about it, do nothing about it, and let it fester over time. In this passage Yeshua does something intentionally dramatic to clean house. He makes an example of the money changers.

You personally do not have to make a huge fuss, and turn over tables in order to set things right. But you should, in the quiet of your heart, ask the Lord to drive out all those things which pollute your relationship with him.

DECEMBER 4

We often picture God as benevolent, above it all, and somewhat passive regarding the small affairs of humankind. But nothing could be further from the truth. God is highly interested in the small goings-on of our daily lives. He is not passive and soft in the area of holiness. So let him calm your heart today, and meet you in your prayer time. In your stillness, consider how un-quiet Yeshua was as he cleaned out the Temple.

And his disciples remembered that it is written: Zeal for your house will consume me.

✡ *John 2:17*

The house of God in the Bible represents some amazing typology. In the old days it was a physical structure given by God to allow his sinful people to approach him. In the time of Yeshua it had become a corrupt institution. Even still, he cared greatly for it, because it stood as a physical representation of the inner life of his people.

Today, *you* have become his house, as the Holy Spirit lives inside you. How much more then, should you be zealous to keep your own house in order? Ask God once again to 'clean house!' "Dear Lord, I cannot do this myself, only you can clean me up. Please cleanse me of…"

DECEMBER 5

The mighty power of God is such that nothing can stand in his way. Not even death or taxes. Yeshua was able to raise himself from the dead, and he can, and will, do the same for you. His disciples understood this only after he had proclaimed it, and then proven it.

Jesus answered, "Destroy this temple, and I will raise it up in three days."

But he was speaking about the temple of his body.

✡*John 2:19,21*

If the body of Yeshua was a temple of God, then your body too is a temple of the Holy Spirit. God cares about your physical body – what you put into it, and how you treat it.

As a child of the living Lord, you are an enfleshed soul. When God raises you, he will also raise your body. No believer can expect to live in eternity without a body, because God created us to have physical bodies.

Today then, present yourself to him entirely. Give Yeshua the totality of who you are in prayer.

DECEMBER 6

In his boldness, Yeshua drove a whole business class out of the temple of God. This was not simply done out of anger, but it was an intense symbolic action, similar to Moses smashing the tablets at the foot of Mount Sinai, after finding the children of Israel with a golden calf idol. The act represented God's thoughts and emotions concerning spiritual purity, fidelity to the covenant promises, and loyalty to the Lord. But these actions are ultimately meant to bring people to faith.

Likewise, and even more so, the resurrection of Yeshua is a sure sign, meant to call people to put their faith in him.

So when he was raised from the dead, his disciples remembered that he had said this, and they believed the Scripture and the statement Jesus had made.

✡ *John 2:22*

The Gospel of John is really a book of signs, each one meant to demonstrate that Yeshua is Lord. There is not a single believer who would not give anything to have seen Yeshua raised from the dead. Yet, our trust in him is based on what he has done, not on our own wishes or demands. Hence, if the Lord says he will return, he will, and God has never broken a promise.

Take that to heart today as you pray. In all of history, he has never broken a single solitary promise.

<u>DECEMBER 7</u>

As your day unfolds, turn your thoughts again to the Holy One, who rules the universe, and also cares for you like a shepherd. He is more than able to help you in times of need. Consider his over-arching power.

"To whom will you compare me, or who is my equal?" asks the Holy One. Look up and see! Who created these?
He brings out the stars by number; he calls all of them by name. Because of his great power and strength, not one of them is missing.

✡ *Isaiah 40:25-26*

If none of the stars are missing, and the stars themselves are incalculable to our greatest scientific minds, doesn't that mean he also knows your personal circumstances as well?

No matter what you are dealing with, let him help you. Walk with him, and he will carry you through it. Praise him in your pain, and he will comfort you with his abiding shalom. May your prayers be filled with his thoughts, and may his will be done in your life today.

DECEMBER 8

The Lord is not fooled by anything. He knows exactly what happens behind every closed door, in every private room, and there are no secrets kept from him. God does not believe in conspiracy theories, because he doesn't need to speculate! He knows the absolute Truth in every situation. Do not be afraid to let God go deeply into your private life, to heal you, and to give you strength for the days ahead.

Jesus, however, would not entrust himself to them, since he knew them all, and because he did not need anyone to testify about man; for he himself knew what was in man.

✡ *John 2:24-25*

Just because God knows you better than you know yourself, does not mean he is bent on harming you. Quite the contrary. He has your best interests at heart.

The Lord wants you to approach him as a beloved child, with eagerness and joy. Do not think your sin disqualifies you from coming to Yeshua. He already knows what is inside you, and he wants you to come to him anyway, so that he can heal you from the inside.

<u>DECEMBER 9</u>

God loves living things. He loves *life*. An all-important part of being human, living as creatures made in God's image, is not distancing ourselves from the basic truths of who we really are. We de-humanize ourselves when we attempt to live apart from God. In light of this, pray today for a deeper sense of connection with the Lord, and an awareness of who you are in Yeshua. Who are you in the following short section?

I am the true vine, and my Father is the gardener. Every branch in me that does not produce fruit he removes, and he prunes every branch that produces fruit so that it will produce more fruit.

✡ *John 15:1-2*

A person who tends to greenery is well aware of the care required to cultivate a healthy plant. Note how God *tends* to his children in this passage, like the living, growing creatures we are. But not every branch is fit for Kingdom life, and many get discarded for lack of fruit. Pray about this today.

Does this imagery make you willing to pray that God would indeed *prune* you, if necessary, cutting off what does not belong? If this is a struggle, start your prayer along these lines: "Dear God, I don't like pain, and I don't enjoy pruning, but I know you are determined to produce fruit in my life. Please help me submit to your will today as I..."

DECEMBER 10

Once again you have an opportunity to connect with God, refresh your soul, and be filled with the Spirit. Don't miss out! Take seriously your time with him, because he cares deeply about you. If you neglect your devotional life, you will soon find yourself running on empty, wondering where God is, and not knowing why you feel so ill at ease.

Remain in me, and I in you. Just as a branch is unable to produce fruit by itself unless it remains on the vine, neither can you unless you remain in me.

✡ *John 15:4*

Yeshua asks you to remain, or stay *in* him. He is *inside* of us, through the Holy Spirit. Yet your ability to remain in him is based on *his* power to hold onto you. We are responsible to continue walking with Yeshua, by making time to pray, and reading his word. But to remain in him means to *rest* in him as well.

Have you been busy, stressed, overwhelmed? (Who hasn't?) He calls you to remain and rest in him, and that is something *he* empowers you to do. That is all he requires of you. "Dear Lord help me simply to remain in you today…"

<u>DECEMBER 11</u>

Apart from God, our lives have no meaning, and what's more, we have only a tragic destiny in our future if we reject Yeshua. He is the source and sustenance for our lives. The only way to live, is to live in him. All other paths lead to destruction.

I am the vine; you are the branches. The one who remains in me and I in him produces much fruit, because you can do nothing without me. If anyone does not remain in me, he is thrown aside like a branch and he withers. They gather them, throw them into the fire, and they are burned.

✡ *John 15:5-6*

The Kingdom of God is growing, increasing, and spreading throughout all creation. One day it will saturate everything, so that nothing exists which is not entirely dedicated to life in the presence of God. Whatever remains outside, will be thrown into the fire.

The picture of a vine is meant to cause us to understand how utterly dependent we are on him. It is a warning, but also an encouragement. All you need to do, is plant your roots deep in his word, dedicate your life to him, and allow him to grow you into the person you are meant to be. This means accepting the limits he sets, while embracing the growth he causes. Go to him in prayer over these things today.

DECEMBER 12

God has it in mind to bless you, fully. He has set divine ideas and plans in motion to bring this world, and you along with it, to a greater reality. You need only draw close to him, and stay there. If God did not love you so, he would not have sent his Son to die for you. And if Yeshua had not loved you so, he would not have died and risen again to show you the way. You are cherished and dearly loved by God Almighty, and as such, everything he has to offer is yours.

If you remain in me and my words remain in you, ask whatever you want and it will be done for you. My Father is glorified by this: that you produce much fruit and prove to be my disciples.

✡ *John 15:7-8*

Do not lose sight of the fact that God has set boundaries, wise limitations, on what he will allow in this world. For example, he will not allow the devil to prevail, he will not allow a flood to wash humanity away again, and similarly he will not allow you to have things which would harm you beyond his good will for your life. But if you pray to God asking him to cause you flourish in his Kingdom, he will shower all blessings on you. Do that today!

DECEMBER 13

Your spiritual life is inordinately serious, even if it doesn't always cross your mind. You may be concerned with your physical health, your emotions, and many other things, but your spiritual well-being is crucial to your eternal standing. A person you neglects the spiritual life, will lose everything. As Yeshua said, "Apart from me you can do nothing." That is why sticking close to God is not optional, it is a command to all of humanity.

As the Father has loved me, I have also loved you. Remain in my love.

✡ *John 15:9*

Based on the fact that God loves you, it is imperative that you let God *continue* to love you. You do this by accepting his love, and admitting your desperate need of it, then loving others. There is no law against *love*.

You may *remain* in his love by living a life that reflects obedience to his commands – doing what he says to do. But this does not mean living under the legal requirements of the Torah; it means showing *love* the way he does – by laying down your life for other people. That is how you remain in his love, and that is what his desire is for you.

You can begin that today by praying like this, "Loving Lord, I want to love people the way Yeshua did. Please help me today, to put other people ahead of myself by…"

<u>DECEMBER 14</u>

The Day of the Lord will be like a great family reunion. The people who lived far from each other, those who missed each other, and those who lost loved ones in wars – all those who follow Yeshua will be reunited in a heavenly gathering.

Raise your eyes and look around: they all gather and come to you; your sons will come from far away, and your daughters on the hips of nannies.

✡ *Isaiah 60:4*

This picture from Isaiah is speaking to an Israel who has lost her ability to bear children, but miraculously, they will come springing up from everywhere. Men and women, infants, and grandparents, all will make the great journey to a restored Israel, where Yeshua will receive his family.

Today after you pray, lift up your eyes and look around. You might begin with, "Dear God I want to see your glory, and be part of the family of Yeshua…"

<u>DECEMBER 15</u>

The promises of God are sweet and wonderful. In Scripture, we get a picture of a hopeful future, filled with great blessing and joy. Passages like the one below are meant to entice our imagination, and spur us on to action. Take these words to heart, as instructions to God's people, Israel, to walk in boldness, humility, and faith.

Enlarge the site of your tent, and let your tent curtains be stretched out; do not hold back; lengthen your ropes, and drive your pegs deep. For you will spread out to the right and to the left, and your descendants will dispossess nations and inhabit the desolate cities.

✡*Isaiah 54:2-3*

In your prayer time today, pray about your own 'tent.' What would it mean in your life, if you made it a little bigger, and stretched it out a bit? Are there areas in which your perspective may be too small? (Smaller than God would want for you?)

Pray for wisdom now, and ask the Lord to show you ways in which he would want you to grow, and not hold back.

<u>DECEMBER 16</u>

Most of the people who are open-hearted toward Yeshua simply want to know if he is for real. They are not necessarily looking at you to find out if *you* are a sinner. (They already know you are!) A person with an angry or closed heart will look at you with accusation and scorn once you are proven to be a flawed human being. But people who are truly searching for God simply want to know if *his* grace is genuine or not. In answer to that, God calls us to consider the invitation he is extending.

"Come, let's settle this," says the Lord. "Though your sins are scarlet, they will be as white as snow; though they are crimson red, they will be like wool.

✡ *Isaiah 1:18*

Isn't the idea of *purity* and *perfection* alluring enough to make a person want to come to Yeshua? It ought to be. What are the alternatives? To remain dirty, fallen, and broken. But that's not what God wants for you, or for anybody. The Lord is calling us to be reasonable and rational about our situation: "Come! Let us reason together!"

If we give our lives to him entirely, walking in obedience to his character, then he will take care of the rest. Praise God!

<u>DECEMBER 17</u>

On some level, your relationship with God is reflective of your relationship with any other person in your life. To some degree, we all wrestle with each other, and God is not above having person emotion deeply invested into his relationship with you.

I deserted you for a brief moment, but I will take you back with abundant compassion.

✡ *Isaiah 54:7*

We resemble God in some ways, for example, we all have emotions. But God is not like us, in that he is perfectly merciful. He does not let mere feelings dictate his mercy, rather, he is guided by his *character*, which is perfect in justice and morality.

One day, in tears of joy, you will be able to thank him face to face. But why wait? You can praise him today, right where you are.

DECEMBER 18

Unlike mankind, God does not ever fall short of perfection. That may make it seem as if God is distant, out of our reach, and untouchable. But he allows us to approach him through Yeshua, and through prayer. You have full access to the Lord, because he is kind. And when he expresses anger, or gentle compassion, it comes from a place of holiness and righteousness. In other words, unlike our emotions, God is always perfectly justified in his anger, or sorrow, or joy.

In a surge of anger I hid my face from you for a moment, but I will have compassion on you with everlasting love,"
says the Lord your Redeemer.

✡ *Isaiah 54:8*

At the end of the day, God knows we are unable to see things from his vantage point. He knows we have a limited understanding as well. For that reason, he is quick to forgive. He is also justified in having high hopes for us, because he knows our true potential.

When he turns to you with a forgiving heart, it is because he loves you, and knows you are weak, and in need of help. When you pray to him today, he will welcome you. Ask God to help you understand your own emotions, and his. Ask him to make your heart conform to his. When you are in alignment with God, you will weep over the same things he weeps over, and rejoice over the same things he does.

<u>DECEMBER 19</u>

At the end of all things, the world and the universe itself will be reconstituted. It will be both renewed and restored, to the ideal peace which only God can produce. But there will be a sort of cosmic cleaning when that happens, which will involve old things being swept away, leaving only that which can stand for eternity future.

For this is like the days of Noah to me: when I swore that the water of Noah would never flood the earth again, so I have sworn that I will not be angry with you or rebuke you.

✡ *Isaiah 54:9*

In this passage God is speaking to Israel, heavenly Israel, which will exist for eternity. Thanks to Yeshua, this includes you. But even though there will never be another flood to bring judgment on the earth, there will be a fire. It won't be water next time.

In your devotional time today, ask God to increase your understanding of his ways, and to prepare you for life in the world you live in currently. "Dear God, I need you with me as I do the things you've called me to today. Please lift my eyes up to see what you are bringing, and help me walk towards you as I…"

<u>DECEMBER 20</u>

God promises to give you peace through Yeshua. What a great blessing this promise is, especially living in a war torn world, which is at odds with God himself! And consider how strong his commitment is to this very thing…

Though the mountains move and the hills shake, my love will not be removed from you and my covenant of peace will not be shaken," says your compassionate Lord.

✡ *Isaiah 54:10*

Whatever may befall the earth, he will hold you up. The stars may fall from the sky, but he will sustain you. Death may destroy your body, but he will redeem you from the grave. His love is all-powerful, and his promise is firm and secure.

Tell him all your thoughts and concerns, even the little things. He is in it all.

__DECEMBER 21__

Prayer can change everything, and more often than not, it changes our hearts. Through prayer and faith in God, things you thought were insurmountable fall into perspective. He will lift your head and help you to see the greater scope of his work, of which you are an important part. Pray today for an ever expanding view of God's overarching purpose. Ask him to guide you and deliver you, as you travel down today's path.

Though the mountains move and the hills shake, my love will not be removed from you and my covenant of peace will not be shaken," says your compassionate Lord.

✡ *Isaiah 54:10*

Life can be confusing. After all, consider what you know as an adult, and how peculiar it all seemed to you as a child. The world is an amazing yet strange place. We live with so many unanswered questions. So take heart today, because God knows about our human limitations. He is most certainly there for you, and has compassion for you. Even if the earth were to shake, his promise of peace would still remain strong.

DECEMBER 22

There are many spiritual pitfalls in today's world, and in western society religion has been turned upside down in so many ways. When you think about modern religious leadership, what comes to mind? Power? Money? Corruption? Think on the words of Moses…

You may say to yourself, 'How can we recognize a message the Lord has not spoken? ' When a prophet speaks in the Lord's name, and the message does not come true or is not fulfilled, that is a message the Lord has not spoken. The prophet has spoken it presumptuously. Do not be afraid of him.

✡ *Deuteronomy 18:21-22*

We are called to test everything we hear against the word of God. If a preacher claims to have a message from the Lord, but it is not in line with biblical truth, then don't let it hinder you. Move on. *Where there is much talk, there is sin!*

As for you, seek the face of Yeshua every day, and you will never be lead astray. Through him, you have a direct connection to the God who created the universe!

DECEMBER 23

How many choices do we make in a day? Hundreds? Thousands? Sometimes a dilemma presents itself, and we are torn over what to do. When you wrestle with right and wrong, and make the tough decision to do the *right* thing, no matter what may come of it, you have been dealing with *ethics* – the practice of right behavior. The Lord has much to say about ethical problems.

Do not deny justice or show partiality to anyone. Do not accept a bribe, for it blinds the eyes of the wise and twists the words of the righteous.

✡ *Deuteronomy 16:19*

In our fallen world it can sometimes be difficult to determine right from wrong, mostly because our fallen nature clouds our judgment. But deep down inside, you will know the difference if you let God shape your ethics.

God will speak to you clearly when you seek to do what is right. Do not deny him, and pretend not to hear. God will honor your best attempts to follow his morality. He will also show you mercy when you seek forgiveness after you mess up. Over time, he will also strengthen you, to do what is right, and walk the way Yeshua did, even when it is extremely difficult.

DECEMBER 24

The most important decision of your life, is the choice to turn toward God. Only through the crosswork of Yeshua can you receive forgiveness for your sins. Then all the ups and downs you experience have meaning in him. But apart from Yeshua we are entirely lost, untethered, and drifting alone on the open seas. So turning to him is paramount. And a big part of the faithwalk is remembering that you need to continue to look to him, again and again.

Therefore produce fruit consistent with repentance.

✡ *Matthew 3:8*

Fruit grows through seasons, and as a result of sunshine, water, good soil, cultivation, and time. In other words, fruit production does not happen in a single instant. You cannot expect to turn to Yeshua, and spontaneously arrive at your final destination of heavenly glory. It takes time! And turning to him, *repenting*, should be a regular practice in the life of every believer.

Just like a fruit tree needs support over time, you need to repent whenever you feel convicted in your heart. That is what allows your life to flourish before him, so that you can stand on solid ground, rooted in his truth, not tossed about on the crashing waves.

DECEMBER 25

It may be difficult to hear, but nothing about a person can earn God's favor. Absolutely nothing commends you to him. We may have highly influential friends, lots of money, amazing talents, and any variety of skills and successes in life. Nothing at all, not even a gold plated V.I.P. pass can impress God. What impresses him is your simple trust in Yeshua.

And don't presume to say to yourselves, 'We have Abraham as our father.' For I tell you that God is able to raise up children for Abraham from these stones.

✡ *Matthew 3:9*

Even the nicest, sweetest, most kindly person can be spiritually arrogant toward God. It's all a matter of the heart. You may be a child of Abraham, a well-educated doctor, an expert in theology and law, and an all-around nice guy or girl with a high class pedigree, but God does not need your accolades.

He wants your trust, your heart, and your complete devotion. Is that because he is insecure? Not at all. He wants your worship because he is worthy of it, for all the best reasons. Praise him in your prayer time today, because he has generously shown you the path of eternal life.

DECEMBER 26

The religious leaders of Yeshua's day were wedded to the idea that outward behavior was the key to spiritual blessing. They were mistaken. Nobody comes to God accept through faith in Yeshua, the true Messiah. When you put your life in his hands, looking to his crosswork for your salvation, he fills you with the Holy Spirit, as a promise of heaven.

I baptize you with water for repentance, but the one who is coming after me is more powerful than I. I am not worthy to remove his sandals. He himself will baptize you with the Holy Spirit and fire. His winnowing shovel is in his hand, and he will clear his threshing floor and gather his wheat into the barn. But the chaff he will burn with fire that never goes out.

✡ *Matthew 3:11-12*

The Holy Spirit is your guarantee of salvation, your eternal security. Being filled with the Spirit means you are marked out for mercy, when Judgment Day comes. The fire of God's judgment will not destroy you, rather, it will prove your composition, that you are indeed a child of God through Yeshua.

The very same Day will be a disaster for some people, but a celebration for God's people. Prepare your heart in prayer for the road ahead. You have miles to go yet, before reaching the realm of the Kingdom of God.

DECEMBER 27

When you come before the Lord, you are entering into closeness with the most powerful Being in the universe. He is a friend to you, through Yeshua, and sees you as his son or daughter. Nobody in all of creation can steal you away from him. No matter what happens to you, nothing is beyond his reach or control. And because he is all-powerful, even the most terrible things are no genuine threat to your eternity.

Look, I have created the craftsman who blows on the charcoal fire and produces a weapon suitable for its task; and I have created the destroyer to cause havoc.

✡ *Isaiah 54:16*

If God created the world, he is also the bringer of danger. We do not live in a safe world, although God could have made it differently if he had wanted to. Death is a result of The Fall, but there is also something to be said for the notion that God was not at all surprised by sin, and that he knew full well what the outcome would be. As for us, we can take great comfort in the fact that he will protect us from the ultimate destruction – the grave.

Do you have a hard time with 'grey areas' of life? Nothing catches God by surprise. Look to him in times of stress and trouble. He will give you crystal clarity over time. Don't give up! Prayer is a daily discipline.

DECEMBER 28

God is the Creator and Master over all things.
There is nothing on earth or in heaven, not a speck
of dust nor a blazing star, which is not his own. As
we scrape out our existences here in this world, we
tend to fight over earthly things, like money, food,
and power. But the Lord sees all of that, and
encourages us to simply trust in him. He owns
everything, and there is no shortage of any kind
with Yeshua.

*Come, everyone who is thirsty, come to the water;
and you without silver, come, buy, and eat! Come,
buy wine and milk without silver and without cost!*

✡ *Isaiah 55:1*

This sweet verse from Isaiah indicates that God is in
the business of providence. We may see poverty
today, but one day all things will be new, and
nobody will go hungry or thirst ever again. He will
give it away for free! And what's more, he is
already giving the invitation, through faith in
Yeshua. Your sins have been paid for, and he
forgives you freely. You need only ask him into
your heart.

Do so once again, today, in your prayer time.
Accept his invitation to drink and eat without cost.

<u>DECEMBER 29</u>

Yeshua is the fulfillment of all prophecy. The Scriptures illustrate and teach the personhood of Yeshua from every point of view imaginable. He is all in all. That is why he could stand boldly and proclaim the verses from Isaiah for himself. Both Isaiah and Yeshua invite you to come down to the riverside, and have your sins washed away.

On the last and most important day of the festival, Jesus stood up and cried out, "If anyone is thirsty, let him come to me and drink. The one who believes in me, as the Scripture has said, will have streams of living water flow from deep within him."

✡ *John 7:37-38*

If God is in the business of providing for people, and freely forgiving sins, then it is an open invitation that still stands. Anyone who is thirsty can come to him, even now.

Are you thirsty for the waters of heaven? Recommit yourself to Yeshua, and he will cause a fountain of life to come up from within your heart. You will have hope during this life, and indescribably joy in the next.

DECEMBER 30

While the invitation to come to Yeshua is open, it will not always be so. There will come a day when the curtain falls, and time is up. The great drama of human history will come to a close, and a new story will be written into eternity. Our present lives are also a reflection of that fact. One day each of us will draw a final breath, and step out of time altogether. That is why the prophet Isaiah exhorts us with a sense of urgency.

Seek the Lord while he may be found;
call to him while he is near.

✡ *Isaiah 55:6*

As you age, day by day, and your body breaks down little by little, it is more important than ever to call upon him. You may be young and vigorous, or you may be growing tired with the passing years, but so long as your heart is beating you still have the chance to call out to him. And don't miss the point of the verse above – he *may still* be found, and he is *already* near. You need only seek him out in prayer.

DECEMBER 31

Sit quietly, close your eyes, take a deep breath, and focus your thoughts on God. He knows you inside and out. Wouldn't it be great to see things from his point of view, just once? Someday our understanding will be greatly expanded, and we will look back on our tiny perspectives of today, and wonder how we ever had such blind spots and limited vision. Well, not to worry. God understands all of that as well…

For my thoughts are not your thoughts, and your ways are not my ways." This is the Lord's declaration. For as heaven is higher than earth, so my ways are higher than your ways, and my thoughts than your thoughts.

✡ *Isaiah 55:8-9*

Truly, there is no comparing ourselves to God. We are made in his image, but we do not share his power, or his wisdom, or even his purity. The reasonings and motives of the Lord are unsearchable to us, and the horizons of his mind are unimaginable. We simply are not capable of 'solving' God, as if he were some puzzle. We are simply fortunate that he has revealed to us what little we can understand, along with what we *need* to know in order to be saved. That is more than enough, although we would always wish to know more.

Trust him today, for a future filled with resolution to all the questions you have ever abandoned.

www.ingramcontent.com/pod-product-compliance
Lightning Source LLC
Chambersburg PA
CBHW021418150726
47989CB00001B/24